WORKPLACE BULLYING:

A PHENOMENOLOGICAL STUDY OF ITS EFFECTS ON TARGETS AND ORGANIZATIONAL PRODUCTIVITY

BY

DR. LINDA PROCTOR MATA

i

WORKPLACE BULLYING:
A PHENOMENOLOGICAL STUDY OF ITS EFFECTS ON TARGETS AND ORGANIZATIONAL PRODUCTIVITY

Bennett books may be ordered through booksellers or by contacting:

Bennett Media and Marketing
1603 Capitol Ave., Suite 310 A233
Cheyenne, WY 82001
www.thebennettmediaandmarketing.com
Phone: 1-307-202-9292

Any people depicted in stock imagery provided by Shutterstock are models, and such images are being used for illustrative purposes only.

Certain stock imagery © Shutterstock

ISBN: 978-1-957114-63-7 (Paperback)
ISBN: 978-1-957114-64-4 (eBook)

Printed in the United States of America

BENNETT
MEDIA & MARKETING

PREFACE

Workplace bullying is a global phenomenon that can have detrimental long-term effects on victims. This study reviews the literature on workplace bullying and explores the effects of workplace bullying as perceived by those who have been targeted. Participants in this study describe how bullying has negatively impacted their physical health, psychological health, interpersonal relationships, self-confidence, self-esteem, job satisfaction, and careers. Bullying impedes organizational productivity due to loss of employee morale, employee absenteeism, staff turnover and loss of revenue due to hiring and training of new staff. The Critical Incident Technique was used to conduct in-depth telephone interviews with participants who acknowledged being bullied in the workplace. Findings indicate that bullying is a pervasive problem that appears to be embedded in the culture of the workplace, which can result in a variety of physical and psychological problems that can hinder work performance and impact relationships. If and when victims finally decide to confront the problem, they are unlikely to feel supported by management, who may be knowingly or unknowingly protecting the organizational culture and the perpetrator in order to maintain productivity and the reputation of the company. Moreover, many victims are reluctant to expose the problem because it could jeopardize their job security, well-being, and possibly even exacerbate the problem. The findings presented herein reinforce the need for businesses in both the private and public sector (including the military) to eliminate bullying at all levels of the organization by disseminating and enforcing an unambiguous anti-bullying policy, as well as enhancing communication throughout its various units and divisions that bullying will not be tolerated.

DEDICATION

This book is dedicated to my late parents, Frank and Anabelle Proctor, who always believed in me. I also acknowledge the love of my husband, Robert W. Mata, who has been my side throughout this endeavor and who has never failed to encourage and support me along every step of the way.

Acknowledgements

I would like to first of all acknowledge my school's faculty chair for providing the motivation and encouragement I needed to continue meeting this major achievement. I have encountered many challenges, but with his help I was able to continue to pursue my dream. I would also like to acknowledge support of the two committee members this achievement would not have been possible without their support.

TABLE OF CONTENTS

LIST OF TABLES

LIST OF FIGURES

CHAPTER 1.

INTRODUCTION

Introduction to the Problem

Defining the term "bullying" is a challenge because "agreed-on definitions of bullying do not exist" (Randall, 1997, p. 3). However, Olweus (1993) had earlier suggested a definition that has become commonly-accepted and will be used within the framework of this book. He defined bullying as when a person "… is exposed, repeatedly and over time, to negative actions on the part of one or more other persons, and the victim has difficulty defending himself or herself" (p. 9). Randall (1997) subsequently refined that definition to assert that bullying may not actually have to occur in the form of repeated aggression—that, in fact, the mere fear of repeated aggression may be as detrimental as that initial occurrence. Bullying can and does occur anywhere: at schools, in the military, in families, online (cyber bullying), and in the workplace. This investigation, however, focuses on the latter—bullying in the workplace.

According to The Workplace Bullying Institute (2014), workplace bullying (WB) is similar to other types in that it is health-harming, humiliating, and/or intimidating mistreatment (verbal or non-verbal) of one or more persons (the target) by one or more perpetrators. However, WB differs from other forms in that it is often characterized by work interference or outright sabotage, both of which hinder or prevent work from getting done. Workplace bullying is generally acknowledged as harmful to those targeted and counterproductive to the organization. Moreover, studies have revealed major negative consequences for victims, including loss of self-esteem, a range of deleterious health outcomes, and perhaps even the loss of job or career (Peyton, 2003). In short, WP experts have concluded that deliberate and repeated verbal aggression, coupled with ridicule or harassing and intimidating strategies, can cause mental and physical harm, which they view as a complex phenomenon that can be difficult to address (Davenport, Schwartz, & Eliot, 1999; Hochheiser, 1998; Hornstein, 1996; Malloy, 1998; Namie & Namie, 2003).

According to Namie and Namie (2003), situations in which employees are subjected to verbal attacks and to harassing and intimidating behaviors occur frequently in organizations, causing employees to leave their jobs due to frustration. Unfortunately, the U.S. lags behind other countries in taking steps to address this issue. Moreover, it is still extremely difficult for the victim to find vindication within the court system—although there is a growing number of advocates supporting the cause. In response to this trend, this study explored the phenomenon of bullying in the workplace (i.e., *workplace bullying*). This study is expected to increase public awareness of workplace bullying, perhaps even leading to substantive changes in our legal system that will change these behaviors through increased prosecution.

Background of the Study

Researchers have described with all-too increasing frequency the astounding number of persons in the workplace who have experienced workplace bullying. For example, a report from the Workplace Bullying Institute (WBI) (2014) stated that 49% of all American workers have been affected by workplace bullying—either directly or indirectly. Additionally, Fisher-Blando (2008) reported that nearly 75% of employees surveyed in her research had been affected by workplace bullying, either as a victim or as a witness. Although this phenomenon does not appear to be linked to specific demographic variables (Hoel & Cooper, 2000), gender and ethnicity may play a role in both victimization and predation. For instance, the WBI (2007) reported that women constitute 57% of those bullied, with a slightly higher percentage (60%) of perpetrators reported as being male. Interestingly, however, in 71% of bullying cases it is females victimizing other female workers. The WBI

(2007) also reported victimization statistics according to ethnicity. Specifically, Hispanics were most likely to experience workplace bullying (52%), followed by Blacks (46%), Whites (33.5%), and Asians (30.6%). Similarly, other studies report higher levels of bullying among members of minority groups in comparison to their White colleagues (Hoel & Cooper, 2000).

Workplace bullying is often confused with harassment, but it differs in substantive ways—principally in the frequency of occurrence. Harassment can be defined as any physical or verbal abuse of a person because of their race, religion, age, gender, disability or other legally protected status. "Harassment in the workplace can further be defined as any conduct that creates significant anguish to another person with the intent to bother, scare or emotionally abuse a victim" (Maughan, 2010, para 2). Moreover, harassment may be a single act of aggression. Bullying, on the other hand, is repeated aggression or a pattern of negative acts against a target —or, as has been suggested by Randall (1997), it may manifest itself as fear of repeated aggression.

According to Eliason (1998), increased awareness of legislation prohibiting discrimination may have caused discriminatory acts to become more covert, making discrimination more difficult to identify, prove and tackle. Title VII of the Civil Rights Act of 1964, the Age Discrimination in Employment Act of 1967, the Pregnancy Discrimination Act of 1978, and the Americans with Disabilities Act of 1990 have each created clear, legal protections against harassment. There are, however, few or no uniform and legal safeguards against bullying in the workplace. According to Yamada (2003), legal safeguards for bullying "...must be based primarily on a patchwork of statutory and common law measures governing discrimination, personal injury, wrongful discharge and workplace safety" (p. 400).

What the two share in common, however, is that workplace bullying and harassment both cause frightening and harmful consequences for victims and the organization, resulting in low employee morale, high employee turnover, and lower productivity. Workplace bullying, therefore, needs to be addressed in a more systematic way so that statutes can be put into place that reduce its occurrence. According to Namie (2003), "The time has come to treat workplace bullying the same as sexual harassment or racial discrimination, to identify the perpetrator, establish rules of conduct and penalties and even pass laws prohibiting and penalizing bullying" (p. 1). Namie (2003) further asserts that more research is needed in the area of workplace bullying even though there are an abundance of data and coherent theories.

Statement of the Problem

While workplace bullying presents a tremendous problem to those targeted as victim, it can also negatively impact coworkers who must choose to turn a blind eye or risk retaliation by supporting the victim or reporting the incident. Workplace bullying is also likely to lower organizational productivity (Sepler, 2010), which represents a phenomenon meriting additional research. Indeed, as noted by Einarsen, Hoel, and Cooper (2003), "less attention has been paid to the effects of bullying on organizations than individuals" (p. 145). Unfortunately, it is difficult to assess the costs of bullying to organizations due to factors such as the questionable quality of data and unclear connections between cause and effect (Cooper, Hoel, & Faragher, 2001). According to Tracy, Lutgen-Sandvik, and Alberts, (2006), "Adult bullying at work has a measurable negative impact on organizations. Direct costs include increased disability workers' compensation claims and increased medical costs" (p. 153)—not to mention the costs associated with wrongful discharge (Bassman, 1992) and resulting lawsuits (Matusewitch, 1996; Yamada, 2000). Additionally, Pryor (1987) stated that organizations incur direct costs resulting from workplace bullying that relate to sick leave, turnover, reduced productivity and potential litigation. Indirect costs include low quality work, reduced productivity and high staff turnover. According to Harrison Psychological Associates (2002), business costs to employers resulting from bullying and harassment of employees totaled more than $180 million over a two-year period of their study. Rayner and Keashly (2004) estimated that replacement costs of those who leave as a result of having being bullied or witnessing bullying total about $1.2 million per year for organizations averaging 1000 employees.

In short, workplace bullying is a serious and dynamic problem with far-reaching consequences that should be of interest to managers, consultants, human resource professionals, and, of course, to the victims themselves. To substantively address the problem of bullying, increased research is need to explore the concept, causes, and nature of the phenomenon. Indeed, as Giorgi (2009) asserted: "Despite the abundance of data and the development of coherent theories, more research seems needed concerning the causes of workplace bullying" (p. 35). Although a number of empirical studies have been conducted to examine the correlation between bullying and the dynamics of the various work environments, few studies have discussed in detail the organizational mechanics behind bullying—i.e., how and why these conditions and processes may contribute to it (Salin, 2003). In military research, there have been few studies on bullying (Nils, Lau, Ruse, & Moen, 2009). This is despite a study among army conscripts in which 12 reported being bullied and 53% observed bullying (Nils et al., 2009). In response to this scholarship deficit, a phenomenological qualitative research study using the Critical Incident Technique was used to solicit data from military veterans who have experienced workplace bullying within and/or outside of the military on how it has impacted their lives.

Purpose of the Study

This study was designed to achieve two goals: (a) to examine how workplace bullying impacts the physical and psychological health, self-esteem, interpersonal relationships, careers and job productivity of victims and bystanders; and (b) to investigate if and how environmental conditions may enable bullying to occur. By examining these issues, the researcher sought to add to the existing knowledge of the complex problems arising from workplace bullying among victims, managers, human resource professionals, consultants, bystanders, witnesses and perpetrators as well.

Rationale

Most studies of bullying have targeted schoolchildren. In contrast, there is limited research about bullying among adults in the workplace. Interest in this topic, however, is growing, and researchers are examining alternative paradigms, as well as combining different methodologies to gain greater understanding of the phenomena (Cowie, Naylor, Rivers, Smith, & Periera, 2002). Continued research is necessary because workplace bullying has such a serious impact on victims, perpetrators, and organizations. Information gathered from this investigation can be used to identify forces in the organization that perpetuate bullying, as well as suggest strategies for eliminating it.

This study focused on the prevalence and myriad impacts of workplace bullying. The inspiration for this study stems from the work of pioneering researchers such as Dr. Heinz Leymann, whose initial research in the 1980s identified some of the side effects of "mobbing" that led to post traumatic stress disorder and, in extreme cases, suicide. Seminal researchers who have extended our knowledge of this pressing issue include Hecker (2007), Westhaus (1998), Zapf (1999), and Tracy (2010). As stated by Tracy et al. (2006), "Identifying the material effects of adult bullying is an important step in persuading organizational policy makers to pay attention to the phenomenon" (p. 150).

Research Questions

This qualitative phenomenological study used first-hand narratives to reveal the impacts of workplace bullying among a small cohort of mostly retired military personnel. In so doing, it was also hoped their responses would also elucidate certain organizational factors (e.g., its culture) contribute to workplace bullying. The following six research questions guided this investigation:

RQ1. How has workplace bullying affected the employee's physical health

RQ2. How has workplace bullying affected the employee's psychological health?

RQ3. How has workplace bullying affected the employee' self-esteem?

RQ4. How has workplace bullying affected the employee's interpersonal relationships?

RQ5. How has workplace bullying affected the employee's job satisfaction and career?

RQ6. How has workplace bullying affected the employee's organizational productivity?

Significance of the Study

The rise of workplace bullying has heightened the need to stem its proliferation and address its many adverse consequences (Canadian Safety Council, 2004). Not only is bullying costly to victims and their families and coworkers, but it also creates an unhealthy workplace, and is detrimental to both the organization and the larger society (Leymann, 1992). This need for across-the-board awareness requires studies that identify perpetrators, suggest rules of workplace conduct (and consequences for failing to adhere to them), and helps employers to develop policies that will reduce the occurrence of bullying (Namie, 2003). This study is expected to contribute to the literature on workplace bullying by addressing its causes from the perspectives of those who have experienced bullying.

Definition of Terms

Compliance Strategies: The rules in an organization that designate what behavior is acceptable or unacceptable.

Harassment: Persistent verbal or physical abuse or torment, which can take on a variety of forms—from bullying in schools and in the workplace to using racial slurs to target an individual or group.

Integrity Strategies: Decision making at every level of the organization formulated, implemented, and addressed in light of a consensual commitment to ethical concerns (Paine, 1994).

Mobbing: An emotional assault on a person by one or more persons after this victim has been identified as a target (Groblinghloff & Becker, 1996).

Norms: Rules that are socially enforced.

Organizational Culture: A system of shared assumptions, values, norms, and artifacts that govern how people behave in an organization.

Self-Esteem: How one perceives his self-worth.

Target: An individual who is the recipient of verbal or physical abuse; usually with the intent of demeaning the individual and/or changing his or her behavior.

Work-related Bullying: Repeated (usually), unreasonable actions directed toward one or more employees that are designed to undermine, humiliate, or intimidate, and which can jeopardize employment and result in a lack of organizational productivity.

Assumptions and Limitations

Most qualitative investigations are designed to explore one or more questions, which are based on certain researcher-held assumptions. For this investigation, information about participants' perceptions of bullying was gathered by interviewing them by telephone. Despite the sensitive nature of the topic, this study assumed that participants would answer candidly and accurately—even though research shows that a significant percentage of bullied targets suffer from physical and/or psychological problems as a result of their victimization (Einarsen & Mikkelson, 2000). This study also assumes that workplace bullying is likely to have a negative impact upon the organization as a whole due to employee absenteeism, employee turnover, lowered productivity, and lessened team performance (Einarsen, 2003). It is further assumed that workplace bullying occurs in the military and produces negative impacts there as in other workplace environments. Finally, it is assumed that the questions developed for this investigation would solicit useful information about the nature of workplace bullying.

Any qualitative study is inherently limited by its reliance on data obtained from human subjects. Given the sensitivity of the topic, therefore, a principal limitation of this study is that participants may be reluctant to fully describe their experiences in a candid, accurate manner—or may not remember events as they actually unfolded. Indeed, as Cowie et al. (2002) noted, "Researchers in the field disagree about the reliability and validity of self-reports on the part of victims, that is the inside perspective on the phenomenon of the bullied person" (p. 35). A related limitation is that there is little information supporting the reliability of human-reported data over time. In some cases, victims' reflections may or may not remain depending on when it occurred. Bjorklund (2004) also indicated that victims might have a reduced ability to process cognitive information, which is evidenced by the fact that participants in his study had a higher error rate in relating to experiences in comparison to a control group. These limitations add fuel to the qualitative fire regarding whether such data can stand up to scrutiny. A final limitation to note is the possibility of researcher bias possibly skewing data interpretation. In other words, validity cannot be assumed; nonetheless the researcher has made every effort to objectively substantiate "how we claim to know what we know" during the data interpretation phase (Altheide & Johnson, 1994, p. 496).

Nature of the Study (or Theoretical Conceptual Framework)

Affective Event
Theory

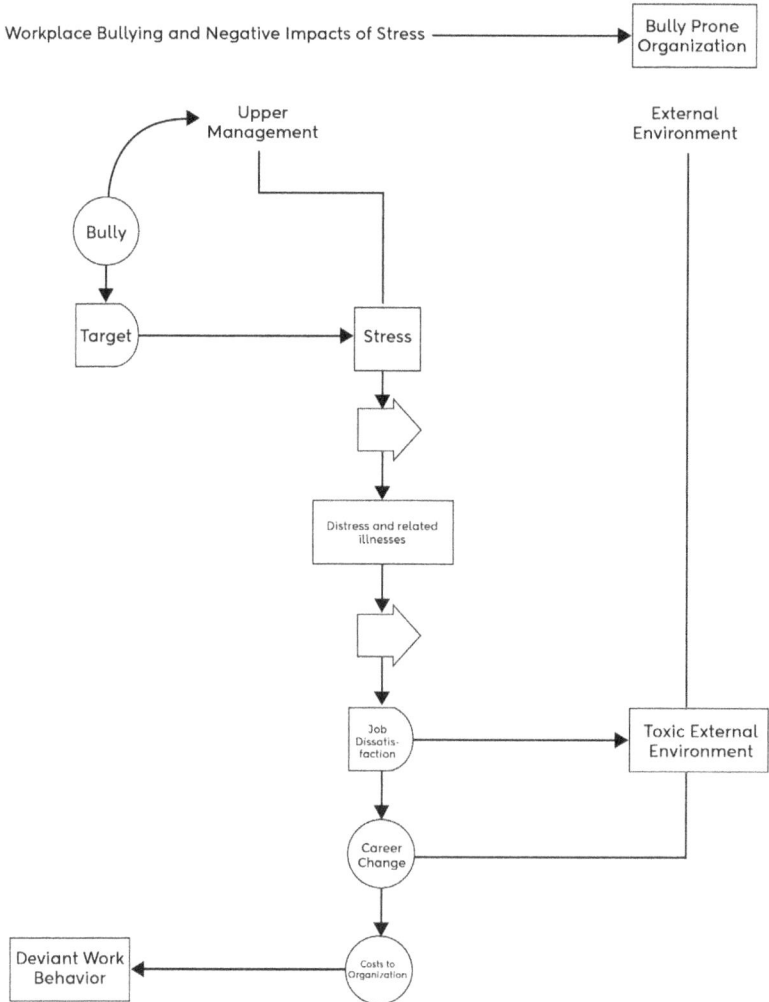

Workplace Bullying and Negative Impacts of Stress ⟶ Bully Prone Organization

Upper Management

External Environment

Bully

Target ⟶ Stress

Distress and related illnesses

Job Dissatisfaction ⟶ Toxic External Environment

Career Change

Deviant Work Behavior ⟵ Costs to Organization

Figure 1. TITLE

10

Organization of the Remainder of the Study

Following this introductory chapter is a literature review (Chapter 2). Chapter 3 details the methodology that the study employed. Chapter 4 provides the results of this investigation, and the final chapter (Chapter 5) discusses implications and recommendations.

CHAPTER 2.

LITERATURE REVIEW

Introduction

Workplace bullying is a serious problem that has the potential to affect workers at all levels of the organization, as indicated below in Figure 2. This phenomenon remains poorly understood—in part because it has been ignored or written off as mere personality conflicts, profiling, or prejudice. Increasingly, however, researchers are beginning to analyze the causes and effects of bullying (Einarsen, Raknes, & Matthiesen, 1994). This increased scrutiny has resulted in a shift from focusing on bullying as a mere interpersonal conflict between the bully, to targeting the ways that organizations contribute to the process of bullying (Einarsen, et al., 2003b).

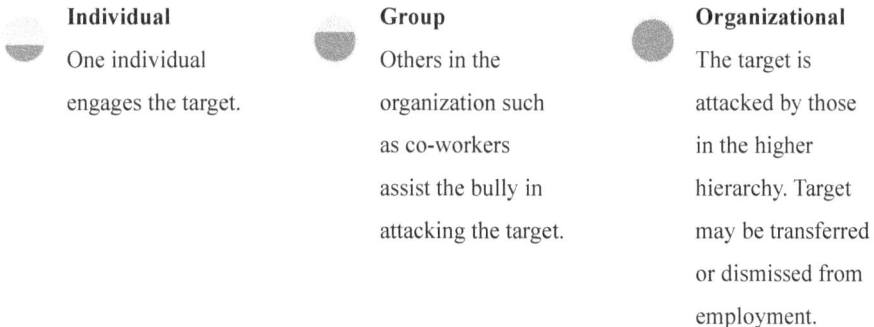

Individual	**Group**	**Organizational**
One individual engages the target.	Others in the organization such as co-workers assist the bully in attacking the target.	The target is attacked by those in the higher hierarchy. Target may be transferred or dismissed from employment.

Figure 2: Levels of Workplace Bullying

Douglas (2001) used the term "workplace abrasion" to describe bullying behavior, arguing that it is not necessarily an issue of intent; in contrast, Randall (1997) defined bullying as "the aggressive behavior arising from the deliberate intent to cause physical or psychological distress to others" (p. 4). Crenshaw (2008), however, reported that many "abrasive" executives are shocked and saddened upon learning of the degree of injury they have inflicted upon others, which rather refutes the notion that they set out to do harm. What is likely is that executives and managers may not fully understand the degree of the injury they caused—even if they deliberately set out to bully an individual in their organization.

Chapter 2 highlights the recent literature on workplace bullying, which can impact the target, human resource professionals, counselors, health care providers, and those who serve in the legal system. Some of the themes that emerged from this investigation are the following:

- Bullying is generally acknowledged to be repeated acts of humiliation against selected targets
- Bullying may be damaging to a victim's physical and psychological health
- Workplace bullying may affect a victim's family members and others in their social network
- Incidences of workplace bullying are rapidly increasing
- Workplace bullying is counterproductive to the organization

The chapter concludes with a discussion of organizational culture, leadership, and bullying in the workplace, including the fact that different organizational cultures favor different styles of leadership that may unintentionally perpetuate the problem. In fact, organizations wishing to eliminate bullying should consider modifying their leadership style and/or organizational culture (Schmmoeller, 2006).

Background/History of the Workplace Bullying Phenomenon

Many states have laws against harassment, but the federal government has passed no comprehensive workplace bullying legislation. Currently, 29 states and 2 territories have introduced the Healthy Workplace Bill, which features employer liability for enabling health-harming and abusive work environments (Dade & Schuering, 2014). It must be noted, however, that as yet no bill impacting private employers has passed into law, and only one bill (which affects Tennessee's public employers) has become law—although it is very limited and grants immunity to employers who have developed anti-workplace bullying policies (Dade & Schuering, 2014).

According to Lutgin-Sandvik (2005), one problem with creating legislation is the lack of an agreed-upon definition for the term "workplace bullying" because the abusive experiences of victims are so varied. This is unlike sexual harassment, which is typically characterized by specific infractions. Moreover, proving bullying and harassment at the workplace can be difficult without a paper-trail or video/audio documentation. Establishing legal charges due to psychological injury for plaintiffs is also difficult. This type of claim is difficult for employers as well, and some claims have been settled out of court (Earnshaw & Morrison, 2001). The issue of funds is "… potentially problematic within this area of law, largely because of the sheer number of costs and the difficulties in obtaining funding or legal aid" (p. 468). Moreover, while the courts may be amenable to awarding damages to plaintiffs, it can be difficult to prove that the injury occurred in the workplace, rather than due to other external sources of stress (Earnshaw & Morrison, 2001). Without financial support from labor unions, the plaintiff may need to seek legal aid, which may be hard to come by.

Psychological harm stemming from various forms of workplace bullying can also be remedied via employment tribunals, which tend to be shorter and are less costly. The employee, however, still has to prove that the bullying occurred (Earnshaw & Morrison, 2001). Plaintiffs have sought relief under the Interactional Infliction of Emotional Distress Law (IIED). However, "an extensive survey and analysis of state case law, concentrating on the period

1995-98, revealed that typical workplace bullying, especially conduct unrelated to sexual harassment or other forms of status-based discrimination, seldom results in liability for IIED" (Yamada, 2004, p. 4). The most frequent reason that courts cited for dismissing the complaints is that the behavior of the alleged bully was "not sufficiently extreme and outrageous" to meet the requirements of the tort. Such formidable hurdles indicate the importance of more awareness of bullying to help prevent it from happening in the first place.

As noted, there has been a growing interest in workplace bullying by the media, and in both popular and scholarly journals. In the literature, bullying is often described in terms of frequency and duration of the behavior. It is further identified by "...the reaction of the target, balance of power between parties and the interest of the perpetrator" (Hoel, Rayner, & Cooper, 1999, pp. 56-57). Compounding the complexity of creating an operational definition of bullying is that subjective perceptions may be cloudy and/or differ from the experiences of others, which can also minimize its harmful effects. We do know that workplace bullying can be direct or indirect—the former directly targets the victim, while the latter refers to the spillover effects for others in the organization (Rathery, 2005). We may be able to better understand bullying by examining it effects at the organizational level, particularly since according to Liefooghe and Mackenzie-Davey (2001), victims may regard their organizations as promoting bullying.

Brodsky's (1976) seminal book, *The Harassed Worker*, was the first of its kind to address harassment of workers. Brodsky was inspired to expose workplace harassment after reviewing more than a thousand claims filed with the California Workers' Compensation Appeals Board and the Nevada Claims Board by workers who sought compensation due to injuries incurred from workplace harassment (Out, 2005). Brodsky (1976) argued that most of these injuries were preventable. The author was also the first to provide a comprehensive definition of the term "bullying," as follows:

Repeated and persistent attempts by one person to torment, wear down, frustrate, or get a reaction from another person. It is treatment that persistently provokes pressures, frightens, intimidates, or otherwise discomforts another person. The behavior may last for a week or many years. Repeated harassment behavior is felt by the target to place him in a cornered position. He is teased, badgered, insulted and feels he has little recourse to retaliation in kind. (Brodsky, 1976, p. 2)

Einarsen, Raknes, and Mathiesen (1994) later described bullying as a gradually evolving process; however, they noted a difference between bullying and conflict. According to Einarsen (2003a), conflict occurs between two parties of equal power and strength; in contrast, bullying usually occurs when there is a perceived "power imbalance" between two parties and one party feels victimized by the other. Similarly, Zapf and Gross (2001) contended that bullying itself is not conflict; instead, it "… signifies an unresolved social conflict having reached a high level of escalation and an increased imbalance of power" (p. 497). Conflict can naturally emerge from engaging with others where opinions differ; it is not necessarily harmful and disagreements causing conflicts can be resolved constructively. Bullying, on the other hand, is not about resolving disagreements. It is about one gaining power and control over another, which relates to the concept of power and imbalance noted by Einarsen (2003a) and first introduced by Olweus (1991).

Although Olweus (1991) investigated bullying among schoolchildren, many of his discoveries have become integral to studies of workplace bullying. Olweus (1991) asserted that "bullying is behavior that is carried out by one or more people, is marked by an imbalance of power and exposes the target of the bullying repeatedly and overtime to negative actions" (p. 413). When extrapolated to the workplace, the perpetrator is likely to be a manager or supervisor—but could also be a peer whose behavior is supported by management. Bullies usually select targets who possess certain traits, are popular others and have characteristics that workplace bullies wish they had, such as knowledge and competencies (Namie & Namie, 2003; Needham, 2004). Bullies employ their strategies because they can, and they do so with impunity because they either know they will not be punished or they choose to take the risk. In other words, in order for bullying to take place, management must tolerate it (Brodsky, 1976). The result is that thousands of individuals are victimized every day in the workplace (Dilts-Harryman, 2007).

Theories Associated with Bullying Behaviors

Einarsen (2000) remarked that scholarship in the area of workplace bullying has not been grounded in a strong theory base. Indeed, scholars of this phenomenon have found survey instruments and job models to be far more useful in tackling the problem than psycho-social theories that fail to address the dynamics of bullying behaviors at work (Ramsey, 2002). Nonetheless, there are several important theories surrounding the phenomenon of bullying, and each one provides a different lens through which bullying can be viewed and understood. Indeed, bullying is such a complex amalgam of behaviors and so many environmental and psychological factors play into the creation of a bully that one theoretical lens would never be sufficient. Understanding bullying and bullies requires a broader scope tied to established theories that enable researchers to dissect individuals, organizations and cultures for evidence of the practice and factors that perpetuate it.

It should be noted that while there are many theories that would enable researchers to contextualize bullying in a theoretical framework, most of them work best when applied to children and adolescents—or are more applicable in the development of strategies or tools to prevent the behavior or to change an environmental climate.

Ecological Systems Theory

Ecological Systems Theory (EST), which was developed by Urie Bronfenbrenner (1917-2005), posits that human development and human behavior is very much impacted by one's environment—be it family, school, community and the larger societal/cultural landscape (Lee, 2011). This theory is often used to understand the genesis of adolescent bullying in terms of a child's personality traits, home life, level of involvement of the child's parents, the school climate and characteristics of the child's neighborhood and community (Hong, Espelage & Sterzing, 2015). Models based on Ecological Systems Theory will examine the person who is exhibiting bullying behaviors to determine the diverse causes for the behavior so that changes can be made to address the aberrant conduct (Hong et al., 2015).

This theory, while appropriate for studying bullies and their behaviors, is not applicable for use in the current investigation. Given that EST examines multiple realms of developmental influences from one's early years, it is too in-depth, too involved and too much within the realm of psychology, social work and anthropology to be applied to this study of targets of WB. Moreover, this theory is utilized in studies to tease apart the deeper issues that prompt bullying behaviors and is especially useful at revealing a solution. In the adult world within which this study took place, Ecological Systems Theory would be both inappropriate—since the bullies themselves were not involved—and far too invasive to employ.

Social Learning Theory

Bandura and Walters (1963) theorized that learning takes place within a social context and that people learn by observing the behaviors, attitudes and emotional reactions of others. Social Learning Theory (SLT) also speaks to the importance of learning based on observing the system of punishments and rewards that result from certain behaviors. Bosworth and Judkins (2014) investigated the School-wide Positive Behavioral Interventions and Supports (SWPBIS) program, which depends heavily on SLT to alter a school's climate by demonstrating and reinforcing positive behavioral norms. This approach was successful in the schools the researchers studied because it established a climate that promoted positive behavior and mitigated any existing risk for bullying. It did not, however, incorporate any system for punishing problem behaviors. Bosworth and Judkins (2014) indicated that schools that used the program reported fewer incidences of bullying, problem behaviors, and student victimization.

Social Learning Theory does seem to be particularly useful when the focus is on children since their environment is easier to overtly manipulate. What is less certain is the degree to which this theory would be germane the working world of adults where the behavior of bullies could be more deeply ingrained and stem from multiple sources and motivations. Nonetheless, this approach has positive implications for use in the workplace because of its focus on altering the external environment and shifting behaviors in a positive way. Thus, SLT has the potential to be incorporated into any kind of effort to alter unacceptable behaviors and attitudes—even in the adult world if applied in a subtle and reinforced manner.

Social Norms Theory

Thirty years ago, Perkins and Berkowitz (1986) developed their Social Norms Theory (SNT) in association with their investigation of alcohol use patterns among college students. This theory relies on the human desire to fit in—and thus the corresponding need to know what the social norms of a particular group are (Berkowitz, 2004). SNT posits that a person's behavior is impacted by how he or she perceives how other peer group members think and act. Importantly, these perceptions may be overestimated or underestimated, with the former leading to an increased incidence of the behavior, and the latter leading to a decrease in the behavior. SNT has been used to investigate a diverse range of topics—most of them in the public health arena such as tobacco and drug use, but more recently SNT has been applied to reducing prejudicial behaviors and sexual assault. Berkowitz (2004) also noted that Social Norms Theory is very helpful in creating marketing campaigns that tout more desirable social norms and encourage people to curb their less socially acceptable behaviors.

Hingson and Howland (2002) revealed that Social Norms Theory is particularly useful for studying behavioral stimuli among adolescents and young adults. Since this study focuses on older adults, and specifically military veterans, Social Norms Theory was rejected for that reason and because the perspective of this theory is the mitigation or elimination of the undesirable behavior.

Lifestyles Exposure Theory

Within the extensive body of literature on the victims of violence and abuse, there are quite a number of theories that try to explain why a certain person is victimized at a certain time and place. In answer to this inquiry, Hindelang, Gottfredson, and Garofalo (1978) developed their Lifestyle Exposure Theory (LET), which is based on research that shows not everyone has an equal chance to be a victim of crime—but that lifestyle choices make one more vulnerable to being a victim of maltreatment at the hands of others. Garofalo (1986) later expanded this theory by incorporating a victim's psychological propensities toward risk taking. More recently, Sampson and Lauritsen (1994) investigated the extent and frequency of the exposure victims have to their tormentors, along with personal characteristics and victim's prior behavioral choices. The overall message is that curbing lifestyle choices (e.g., frequenting bars and nightclubs in unsavory areas, using illegal substances, heavy alcohol use and participating in illegal activities) will lower a person's risk for being the target of an offender. This theory, while interesting and upholding the intent of this study in examining behavior rather than trying to correct it, is largely concerned with criminal behavior and trying to limit victims' exposure to violent acts by altering lifestyles (Hindelang et al., 1978). It also speaks to the ability to control one's environment, which is clearly not possible for most victims of workplace bullying. Hence, this theory is not germane to this investigation.

Social Dominance Theory

Social Dominance Theory (SDT), which was developed by Sidanius and Pratto (1999), has also been used to try to understand the phenomenon of bullying. SDT focuses on the structure of society—and in particular how human beings have stratified a hierarchy in which some people choose to align their behaviors with social norms and expectations that are rewarded by society and institutions. Sidanius and Pratto (1999) theorized that these hierarchies are supported by the myths and ideologies that encourage the attenuation of inequalities and that the dominant members of society tend to perpetuate those hierarchies. The researchers also argued that group-based inequalities are perpetuated as a result of three principal behaviors among groups: behavioral asymmetry, aggregated individual discrimination, and institutional discrimination. Although aspects of Social Dominance Theory would be useful for understanding bullying in certain institutional settings, is too one-dimensional to be applied in this study and would not be helpful in understanding what effects bullying has on military veterans.

Affective Events Theory

There is one relatively new theory gaining ground in the study of workplace bullying that is more apropos to this study: Affective Events Theory (AET) (Weiss & Cropanzano, 1996). AET provides a structure for investigating the linkages between events that happen in the workplace, emotions, and the range of attitudes and behaviors that stem from those emotions. As such, it is more germane to investigating behaviors that qualify as bullying at work as well as addressing their effects on the targets of WB. Importantly, AET has been empirically tested in both qualitative and quantitative research studies on workplace bullying (Weiss & Cropanzano, 1996). Because AET allows researchers to explore the emotional experiences of employees within the workplace—and situates workplace bullying as less of a particular event or set of events, but as the accrual of negative events (Ashkanasy, 2003)—it is applicable to the current investigation. Therefore, this research study used Affective Events Theory as its theoretical foundation based on its ability to simultaneously explore the how and the why of workplace bullying, as well as the emotional fallout that results from it.

Distinguishing Characteristics of Harassment and Bullying

Harassment

Researchers have noted key differences between bullying and harassment. Harassment is usually associated with targeting an individual or group due to their beliefs or their ethnic/racial categorization or association. On the other hand, targets of bullying are usually identified because of their competence or popularity. Nonetheless, ambiguity remains in defining the two terms.

Under *United States Code* Title 18 Subsection 1514 (a) 1., harassment is defined as "a cause of conduct directed at a specific person that causes substantial emotional distress in such a person and serves no legitimate purpose." Forms of harassment are usually directed toward a target because of his/her legally protected status. Harassment could be characterized by a power disparity and a single negative act can constitute an incident of harassment. The main categories of harassment are age harassment, sexual harassment, race/color harassment, religious harassment, national origin harassment, and disability harassment (HR Direct, 2010).

Harassment can occur via face-to-face communication, written communication, and with telephone and computer communication. Despite the fact that laws have been passed prohibiting harassment due to age, sex, race/color, national origin, disability, etc., there is a rapidly growing subtle form of harassment that is difficult to prosecute under anti- harassment and anti-discrimination laws. Researchers have labeled these covert acts as "microaggressions" or "micro-inequities."

Microaggression. The term microaggression refers to offenses generally directed toward members of various racial and ethnic minorities. The literature suggests that they are currently the most pervasive and harmful forms of discrimination and harassment. For example, "racial microaggression" is defined by " incessant, often gratuitous and subtle offenses" against those of a different race (Davis, 1989, p. 5). According to Sue et al. (2007), racial microaggressions tend to be brief incidences and consist of daily verbal, behavioral, or environmental indignities—whether intentional or unintentional—that communicate hostile, derogatory, or negative racial slights and insults toward people of color. Perpetrators of microaggressions are often unaware that they engage in such communication when they interact with racial/ ethnic minorities. Possible long-term outcomes from acts of microaggression including depression, anxiety, substance abuse disorder and hypertension (Wong, Derthick, Sow, David, & Okazaki, 2014).

Micro-inequities. Sue et al. (2007) defined a micro-inequity as a subtle act of harassment against an individual a business setting due to his or her race and gender. The following scenario is an example of a micro-inequity. A boss walks around the office introducing a new hire to all the current staff members. At each stop, the boss introduces the new hire to new staff while praising their contributions. In contrast, the boss may only mention the target of the micro-inequity by name, while failing to note the accomplishments of that person (Hinton, 2003).

Behaviors such as microaggressions and micro-inequities are difficult to identify as intentional, and their discriminatory effects are difficult to prove even though researchers indicate that they can be more damaging than traditional overt forms of racism (Solorzano, Ceja, & Yosso, 2000). Moreover, civil rights laws designed to combat harassment do not ensure protection against these two forms of harassment. Indeed, there are virtually no studies that point out "… adaptive ways of handling microaggressions by persons of color and suggestions of how to increase the awareness and sensitivity of Whites to microaggressions so that they accept responsibility for their behaviors and for changing them" and change them (Solorzano et al., 2000, p. 65).

The first step in eliminating microaggressions is to stimulate discussion, debate, self-reflection, and helpful dialogue (Sue, 2010). Micro-inequities in the workplace also need to be challenged by employers. Although Rowe (1990) stressed that micro-inequities are usually non-actionable concerns and do not require formal grievances, employers their incidence by being proactive and encourage dialogue on the topic in staff meeting and promote awareness through such measures as attitude surveys. Additionally, workshops can be set up and mentoring programs developed to teach employees how to deal effectively with discrimination.

Bullying

The Workplace Bullying Institute (2014) defined workplace bullying (WB) as repeated, health-harming mistreatment of one or more persons (the targets) by one or more perpetrators. WB is generally agreed to feature one or more of the following three characteristics: (1) verbal abuse; (2) offensive conduct/behaviors (including nonverbal) that are threatening, humiliating or intimidating; and (3) work interference-sabotage that purposefully prevents work from getting done correctly or at all. Zapf & Einarsen (2003) also noted signs of WB, including screaming, cursing, spreading rumors, excessive criticism and destroying a target's property or work. Forms of bullying may also include passive acts such as social ostracism of the victim (Williams & Sommer, 1997)—for example, using the "silent treatment," excluding the person from meetings or gatherings, or ignoring their requests (Rayner, Hoel & Cooper, 2002).

Field (1996) suggested that there are 14 forms of workplace bullying, which are detailed in Table 1.

Table 1.

Field's 14 Forms of Workplace Bullying

Bullying Type	Definition
Serial bullying	The source of the bullying can be traced to one individual who selects one target and then moves on to another after destroying each target. This is probably the most common form of bullying
Secondary bullying	Bullying resulting from the pressure of the serial bully as general behavior starts to decline
Gang bullying or group bullying	A serial bullying with colleagues who all bully or mob a selected individual(s)
Vicarious bullying	Two parties are encouraged to fight. The aggression gets passed around
Regulation bullying	A serial bully forces a target to comply with rules and regulations
Residual bullying	The bullying continues for perhaps years once a bully has left the organization
Legal bullying	The use of vexatious legal action to punish a target
Pressure bullying or unwitting bullying	Having a target work with unrealistic time scales and /or inadequate resources
Corporate bullying	When an employee bullies a target with impunity since laws against bullying do not exist
Institutional bullying	Bullying has been entrenched in the organizational culture
Client bullying	The employee is bullied by those they serve

According to Gardner and Johnson (2001), serial bullying is the most common, but also the most dangerous, type of bullying. In this situation, the bully "… is not merely reacting to stressful or unhealthy workplace conditions but engages in psychological aggression regardless of the circumstances" (p.40).

Serial bullying is usually more difficult to detect because the perpetrators are often introverts who are very intelligent and manipulative (Johnson & Gardner, 2001).

Fox and Stallworth (2005) recently suggested another form of workplace bullying that has some overlap with harassment—namely, "racial and ethnic bullying," or bullying experienced as a result for one's race or membership in an ethnic group. This form contrasts with "general bullying," or bullying that may be experienced by a target regardless of race or ethnicity. However, some researchers still stress that any abuse suffered due to membership in a marginalized racial or ethnic group should solely remain in the domain of harassment.

Einarsen (1999) identified two types of bullying and the conditions where they thrive: "predatory bullying" and "dispute-related bullying." In predatory bullying, the victim has personally done nothing to initiate the bully's attack. The victim spirals—mostly as a result of back luck—into a situation where the predator is demonstrating power or exploiting weaknesses. This type of bullying most often occurs in heavily top-down, authoritarian organizations (e.g., the military or other governmental entities), where (1) the target is singled out and bullied due to membership in a certain group, or (2) perceived as representative of a group or category of people who are disapproved by those in the dominant organizational culture. In short, these employees may be bullied merely for showing up for work (Archer, 1999). Predatory bullying is carried out against those who are perceived of as an easy target; while the perpetrator may be difficult to identify or too powerful/respected to be confronted (Bjorkquist, 1994).

Dispute-related bullying occurs as a result of highly-escalated, unresolved interpersonal conflict (Einarsen, 1999; Leymann, 1999). There is a thin line between interpersonal conflict and bullying. The difference lies in frequency of the aggressor's actions (Leymann, 1996) and in the ability of the subjugated to defend him/herself (Zapf, 1999). Although bullies may be peers or even subordinates, bullying usually exists in situations where there is a power imbalance—e.g., with a superior and a line worker who is forced onto a defenseless position with organizational support backing the bully. The social climate in such instances may escalate into harsh personalized conflict or even office wars. The objective becomes to destroy the opponent (Van de Vliet, 1998). Conflict escalates and a signal is sent throughout the organization possibly indicating that the organization tolerates incivility and rudeness (Namie, 2002, 2003).

Summarized in Table 2 is a list of the key differences between harassment and bullying as suggested by the BullyFreeWorkplace.com (2005). While the two not mutually exclusive (e.g., consider Fox and Stallworth's (2005) description of racial and ethnic bullying), this investigation is concerned with workplace bullying as experienced by a cohort of former military personnel. The rest of this chapter provides a detailed discussion of the complex and growing problem of workplace bullying.

Table 2.

Comparing and Contrasting Harassment and Bullying

Harassment	Bullying
Typically consists of isolated incidences over time	Is very rarely just a single occurrence and happens frequently
The victim realizes he or she is being harassed right away	The victim may not realize what is happening until a pattern becomes clear
If there is an assault, it is usually of a sexual or indecent nature	Almost never consists of assaults of a sexual nature, but mainly physical, such as pushing or punching and often mental abuse
There is often an element of being possessive, for example, stalking a person.	Is usually about controlling the person there and then; for example, frightening someone or making him feel small in front of others
Offensive language relating to the color of one's skin or sex is often used	Swear words can be used, but in a different context and usually to state that one is nonproductive
The problem occurs with the person both in and outside of work	The problem with workplace bullying only occurs in the workplace
The person sees the victim as easy prey	The victim is seen as a threat that must be controlled
The person will often have specific inadequacies in their life such as sexual problems having sexual problems	The bully will be inadequate in all areas of life

Typical Patterns of Bullying

Gardner and Johnson (2001) identified four types of bullies: *the psychopathic bully, the downsizer bully, the top-dog bully, and the serial bully.* The researchers characterized the psychopathic bully as one who bullies due to a need to dominate another because he/she is insecure or presents with some type of personality disorder. The downsizer bully emerged as the result of downsizing activity in the 1980s and 1990s. In other words, managers determined that it was cheaper to "bully away" older workers and replace them with part-time employees or new college graduates who lacked the knowledge and experience—but who were significantly cheaper to employ. The top-dog bully "…causes a 'cascade' of bullying down the system, as board members and top management set the agenda on what is acceptable behavior" (p. 40). The serial bully is perhaps the most insidious of the four, for he or she employs psychological tactics to victimize and subjugate employees. In fact, they are known as "closet bullies" since they are usually not perceived as bullies (ABC Anti-bullying Crusader, 2008). The verbal and emotional abuse could include constant fault-finding, nit-picking, and/or refusing to acknowledge good work. Manipulation and marginalizing are other strategies of the serial bully. Serial bullies generally seek to destroy their target through character assassination since the target is usually a good work performer. Character assassination is achieved through rumors, lies and innuendos used to subjugate or eliminate the target (ABC Anti-bullying Crusader, 2008). The literature suggests that these bullies usually have little or no empathy and once they have eliminated one target, it is not long before they select another target.

Bullying is sometimes mistaken for tough management (Namie & Namie, 2002), but it is not. Rather, it is a phenomenon that creates chaos in organizations at the hands someone who knowingly abuses the rights of others to gain control of a situation and/or the individual(s) involved—typically as one of those four types of bullies described by Gardner and Johnson (2001). Targets may be randomly chosen for any number of reasons, but usually selection is based on the desirable qualities of the target, such as competence, networking skills, and emotional intelligence (Namie & Namie, 2003).

According to the Canadian Safety Council (2000) adult bullies tend to be insecure people with poor or no social skills and little empathy. Their feeling of insecurity are turned outward and used as a weapon to attack and diminish capable people. Tactics used include:

- The target is subjected to unjustified criticism;
- The bully employs trivial fault-finding;
- The target is humiliated, especially in front of others;
- The target is ignored, overruled, isolated, and excluded; and
- The target may be set up for failure by setting unrealistic goals or deadlines, denying necessary information and resources, overloading the target with work or taking all work away (sometimes replacing valuable work with demeaning jobs), or increasing responsibility while removing authority.

The targeted worker receives an unrelenting stream of aggression in order to reduce their performance, self-esteem, and value—all with the goal of terminating their employment. There is also the factor of repeated aggression with the intention of inflicting pain in whatever form the bully selects (Randall, 1977). This repeated aggression is driven by the bully's need to control the victim; in fact, the bullying can escalate to such an extent that it involves others who either voluntarily take part, or are coerced to join the bully in persecuting the victim (Workplace Bullying Institute, 2014).

As Field asserted (1996), "A bullying relationship in the workplace almost always follows a predictable pattern" (p. 34). The bully (usually someone in a supervisory position) will select the target either consciously or unconsciously and begin subjecting him to daily psychological abuse using persistent criticism to win control and undermine the chosen's confidence and self-esteem (Field, 1996). When bullies sense others are observing them, they seek to express justification for their behavior. The target may therefore be placed under scrutiny and inquisition. After some period of time, a trivial incident or minor indiscretion may be identified or invented to use as a basis for disciplinary proceedings. Figure 3 summarizes this pattern of WB.

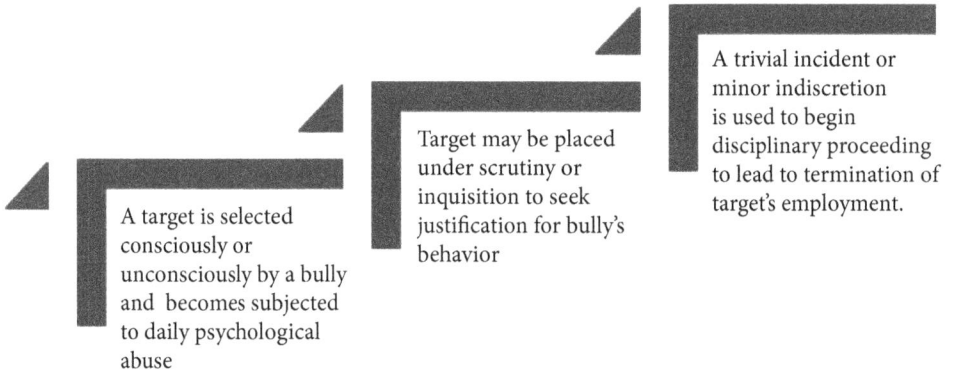

A target is selected consciously or unconsciously by a bully and becomes subjected to daily psychological abuse

Target may be placed under scrutiny or inquisition to seek justification for bully's behavior

A trivial incident or minor indiscretion is used to begin disciplinary proceeding to lead to termination of target's employment.

Figure 3: Field's Predictable Pattern of Bullying Behavior

The bullying takes a toll on victims. "Many targets say that their productivity bottoms out under the stress and eventually they succumb to the physical effects of working in this negative environment" (Rossi, 2006, p.1). Horstein (1996) asserted that the disrespectful behavior produces a toxin that paralyzes its victims, which drains energy, initiative and desire, while also undermining their physical and psychological well-being. The researcher added that targeted subordinates might sometimes transfer those behaviors to their own underlings—while at the same time complaining about their own treatment. As bullies they are categorized as "controllers," while as victims they are identified as s "co-operators."

According to Namie and Namie (2003), values of openness and fair play are viewed as weaknesses by perpetrators. The target may attempt to seek common ground with the bully, but seldom succeeds and eventually is worn down to a defenseless mode, playing into the bully's hand. The target could even have tried to find positive rationale for the behavior levied against them, but the bully is disinterested in making amends and only persists with the objective of eliminating the victim. This feeling of "positional power" may be enhanced in highly-structured organizations that reinforce it for those in supervisory roles. In fact, the bully may actually feel that she has at her disposal the ability to create an organizational climate that harms people (Namie & Namie, 2002). When leadership accepts bullying, an environment of psychological threat is established, which can eventually lead to less corporate productivity with an inhibition of individual and group commitment (Comer & Vega, 2005).

Sometimes the initiating event is a response to provocation—i.e., the victim stands up and asserts his right not to be treated this way. The bully may decide that the victim must now be eliminated, and the person being victimized is subjected to the full force of the employer's disciplinary procedures. A "Jekyll and Hyde" bully will usually have convinced management of her side of the story, thereby being able to further encourage management to use the personnel department as a structural extension of her bullying (Field, 1996). For example, the victim's records may be scanned to gather harmful evidence. "…records are combed for any suitable oversight, omission, inaccuracy or indiscretion. A case is fabricated using words like, 'sub- standard work performance,' 'non-cooperation,' 'insubordination,' and 'gross misconduct'." (Field, 1996, p. 37). These actions may enhance the victim's feelings of insecurity when he/she lacks a sense of support from management. Moreover, bystanders witnessing the event usually cooperate with the bully and remain silent to protect their own interests. In the most extreme cases, an environment of hatred may permeate workplace and is directed toward the victim who becomes increasingly isolated and criticized (Field, 1996).

Bullies may develop more comprehensive plans of attack if they feel a target is too difficult to subjugate. These plans are usually implemented in bully-tolerant organizations. At first, the plan may appear to benefit the victim, but may have been designed to intimidate and control. It may include the "dual-control method," which places one person against another while both are unsure of what is happening. It may also include the addition of "nice-guy intermediary," who may be aware of what is happening but does not want to object for fear of job security (Einarsen, 2003b). The victim now asks himself, "why me?" Issues are not clarified, which can lead to further deterioration of the victim's self-confidence and self-esteem. Victims begin to feel entrapped by a job they love but a superior they hate. They become increasingly worried by the threat of job loss, financial hardship, and the needs of customers, clients and family members. As stress increases, they become more introverted, unable to deduce what is wrong with them (Field, 1996). Eventually victims feel powerless with a sense of "learned helplessness," resulting from the absence or failure of institutional measures to produce outcomes. Such helplessness eventually leads victims to form negative perceptions of the organization as a whole, causing them to give up on efforts to control or rectify the situation (Peterson, Maier, & Seligman, 1995). The suffering of victims may also impact families directly or indirectly; some victims even turn to drugs and alcohol, or in extreme cases become suicidal. Families have been known to breakup due to the stress associated with workplace bullying.

Workplaces that are bully-tolerant become quite pathological and gripped with fear. Everyone, including management, may become too petrified to hold the bully accountable. These workplaces have been described as similar to a *police state* due to prevailing fears. Unconscious norms can become embedded in the culture of the workplace, causing workers to believe that they cannot speak out against bullying. This norm is further compounded by the "norm of silence" (Wyatt & Hare, 1997). Workers may resort to scapegoating a target in order to win acceptance by the group. The scapegoating may even become acute to the point that an individual is targeted and railroaded out of an organization.

The "bully hold," according to Field (1996), tends to comprise dependency, approval, loss of control, isolation, amoral behavior, and fear. Victims respond to this humiliation by reaching out for acceptance and approval. The victim then loses self-control because the perpetrator becomes the determiner of behavior and the victim sees no outlet for their frustration. The bully will not change their objective despite any grievances expressed by the victim or any efforts of the victim to improve work performance. In fact, improving work performance may only make the bully more determined to destroy the victim, especially given the fact that victims are usually selected because of their work strengths. Not only can the victim become the recipient of persistent bullying, but he or she may also receive no rewards or recognition for being a good performer. According to Field (1996) in order to disguise their objectives, bullies may assist victims with enhancing performance for a while, but this assistance is short-lived. In the long-term, the bully comes back to demean the victim's performance.

Bullies may perceive themselves as being immune from accountability because they are seldom held to account for their behavior. Many have long-standing networks in the organization that ensures their position despite their behavior. In addition to receiving management support, they are usually well-liked by others in the workplace. It must be noted, however, that bullies are not necessarily more capable, professional, wise, or knowledgeable than the victim—but they have the support of the organization. At the very least, they certainly lack many of the people skills needed to be fair and objective. As Field (1996) asserted, many have reached their position merely by persuading their superiors that they are the right person for the job, regardless of their ability to do the work.

According to Einarsen and Hoel (2001), bullying is either "work-related" or "personal." Examples of work-related bullying would be giving employees unreasonable deadlines or unmanageable workloads, monitoring the employee's tasks exceedingly, assigning the employee meaningless tasks (or perhaps too little or no tasks at all). Personal bullying includes behavior such as using insulting remarks, exclusive teasing, spreading gossip or rumors, persistent criticism, practical jokes, and intimidation. Any or all of these tactics can cause extreme stress (Zapf, Knory, & Kulla, 1996) and eventually cause harm and damage to the individual (Mikkelsen, Einarsen, & Cooper, 2002).

Stages of Bullying

The frequency and duration of bullying may be as important as the actual nature of the behavior involved (Einarsen, 2000b). Accordingly, Einarsen (1999) described four stages in the bullying process:

- Aggressive behavior
- Bullying
- Stigmatization
- Severe Trauma

Bullying may begin with prejudice and negative stereotypes that lead to labeling the victim as difficult, incompetent, or culpable for a range of work-related problems (Einarsen, 2004). These stereotypes may lead to the first stage of bullying: "aggressive behavior." During this stage, both the victim and the perpetrator acknowledge some degree of frustration between them, but are focused on resolving their differences in a reasonable and constructive manner. The negative acts occurring in this stage are generally discreet and indirect and victims do not perceive themselves as being bullied (Einarsen, 2003).

"Bullying," the second stage in the bullying process, is characterized by more overly negative acts; at this point the victim begins to perceive the bullying. The degree of disagreement and frustration increases between the parties and the conflict escalates. The focus of the frustration changes from resolvable issues to individuals as being the cause of the problems (Einarsen et al., 1994). At this stage the victim begins to experience humiliation, ridicule, and increased isolation Leymann (1990). He or she may also become withdrawn and reluctant to communicate for fear of other further criticism (Field, 1996), causing him or he to be accused of withdrawal, sullenness, not co-operating or communicating, lacking of team spirit, etc. At this point (and later), the victim could turn to alcohol or other substances, putting the person at risk for impaired job performance.

The third stage, "stigmatization," is marked by the victim's display of stress symptoms. These symptoms result from their growing inability to cope with the heightened conflict. The victim may behave irrationally and thus confirm the negative opinions that have been used to characterize her. The victim becomes more frustrated while feeling stigmatized and defenseless against the situation.

The heightened frustration leads to the fourth stage of "trauma." At this point the victim feels that her health, self-image and entire well- being are threatened (Einarsen, 2004). Einarsen (2004) noted that the victim may take extensive sick leave, be granted disability benefits, and in some case be reassigned to another position or even be fired. A key negative act leading to this stage is *ostracism*, which is defined as "the extent to which an individual perceives that he or she is ignored or excluded by others in the workplace" (Ferris, Brown, Berry & Lian, 2008). This workplace ostracism can be intentional or non-intentional (Longzeng, Liqun, & Chun, 2011). A considerable amount of research revealed that ostracism impacts the way people treat and are treated by others (Williams, 2007). Ferris et al. (2008) stated that according to initial evidence, ostracism has a significantly detrimental effect on both employees and organizations. It causes deteriorated psychological well-being (depression, anxiety, emotional exhaustion and unfavorable job attitudes). It also causes workplace deviance and decreased job performance.

Mobbing in the Workplace

Lorenz (1996), who first coined the term "mobbing" (later labeled bullying) observed that certain bird species surround and harass their prey in a manner similar to how humans engage and attack others. Unlike normal conflict, mobbing or bullying is characterized by unethical or bullied actions that are harmful to the entire work environment. Mobbing (i.e., WB) in an organization can spread rapidly and target anyone—rather than focusing on one or more individuals in a discriminatory category of interest (age, gender, race, creed, nationality, disability status, etc.). The bullies will use harassing, abusive, and often terrorizing behavior in an intentional way to force a person out of the workplace. According to Davenport et al. (1999), the psychological consequences of mobbing should be defined as "injury" and not " illness," to reinforce to the role of the perpetrator in inflicting the harm.

"Aggression leading to mobbing is complex and according to common standards of human rights, is an unethical disorder of communication and an extreme psychological stressor" (Groeblinghoff & Becker, 1996, p. 278), that can lead to either/both severe psychological and physical illnesses. The risks to victim are escalated when he/she lacks alternatives (e.g., a change of workplace) or has additional problems in private life (Lazarus & Folkman, 1984). Victims of mobbing often have to leave their jobs in disability status. In extreme cases, and after long periods of illness or social isolation, the victim may even commit suicide.

A "mobber" will typically first strike at the victim via an emotional assault to create an emotional reaction. The bully will then manipulate the target's co-workers into feeling privileged to be in his/her confidence. The bully feigns concern for the target while suggesting with lies and twisted information that the target has in some way offended him/her. The co-workers then support the attacks upon the target due to loyalty for the bully boss (ABC Anti-Bullying Crusader, 2008).

According to Leymann (1996), bullying or mobbing can be categorized into five broad categories: (1) attacks to one's reputation, (2) attacks to one's work performance, (3) attacks to one's self-expression and the way communication happens, (4) attacks to one's social relations/circumstances, and (5) attacks to one's physical, emotional, and psychological health. Table 3 lists these areas and the related bullying behaviors that characterize them.

Table 3

Acts of Leymann's Inventory of Psychological Terror: Categories and Behaviors

ATTACKS ON REPUTATION

People talk badly behind your back

You are ridiculed

You are forced to undergo a psychiatric evaluation or examination

A handicapped is ridiculed

Unfounded rumors are circulated

You are treated as if you are mentally ill

Your efforts are judged in the wrong way

People imitate your gestures, walk or voice

Your private life is ridiculed

Your personal life, political or religious beliefs are ridiculed

You are forced to do a job that negatively impacts your self-esteem

Your decisions are always questioned

You endure textual innuendoes

You are called demeaning names

ATTACKS ON WORK PERFORMANCE

There are no special tasks for you

Corollary damage creates financial costs for you

Supervisor take away assignments so you cannot even invent new tasks

You are interrupted constantly

Supervisor restricts the opportunity for you to express yourself

Colleagues/co-workers restrict your opportunity to express yourself

You are given tasks that are way beyond your qualifications in order to discredit you

You are given meaningless jobs to carry out

ATTACKS ON COMMUNICATION

You are yelled at and loudly scolded

Your work is constantly criticized

Our threats are made

Written threats are made

There is constant criticism about your private life

Contact is denied through innuendoes

You are terrorized on the telephone

Contact is denied through looks are gestures

ATTACKS ON SOCIAL CIRCUMSTANCES
People do not speak with you anymore
Colleagues are forbidden to talk to you
You cannot talk to anyone (i.e., access to others is denied)
You are treated as if you are invisible
You are put into a workplace that is isolated from others

ATTACKS OF THREAT OR REAL PHYSICAL COERCION
You are forced to do a physically strenuous job
You are the object of physical abuse or outright sexual harassment
Light violence is used to threaten you

List of activities cited above is adapted from Leymann (1996)

Leymann (1993) also delineated the five phases of the mobbing process: (1) a conflict or critical incident occurs, which may not be work-related; (2) aggressive acts and psychological assaults set the mobbing dynamic into motion; (3) management supports these assaults on the victim by extending support to the perpetrator and begins the isolation and expulsion process; (4) the victim is labeled as difficult or mentally ill, which almost always leads to expulsion or resignation; and (5) the victim may develop PTSD or psychometric illness. Mobbing has been called a "syndrome" because like its namesake it consists of numerous factors occurring simultaneously with the goal of humiliating and subduing an individual. It is a "ganging up" by the leader(s), organization, superior, co-workers, or subordinates who rally others into systematic and frequent mob-like behavior. The organization then generally ignores, condones, and in some cases, instigates the behavior (Davenport et al., 1999).

There are three degrees of mobbing (Davenport et al., 1999), each of which corresponds to successive impacts on those being mobbed. These degrees are determined by the intensity, duration, and frequency of the mobbing, the psychology of the mobbed individuals, their upbringing, past experience, and general circumstances. According to Davenport et al. (1999) in the first degree, the victim manages to resist, escapes at an early stage, or is fully rehabilitated in the same workplace or somewhere else. In the second degree, the affected person cannot immediately of escape at all; in this stage the victim suffers temporary or prolonged mental and/or physical disability, and has difficulty reentering the workplace. In the final stage, the affected person is unable to re-enter the workforce. The physical and mental injuries are such that rehabilitation seems unlikely, unless a very specialized treatment protocol is applied.

Mobbing not only affects one's dignity, integrity, credibility, and professional competence, but may affect one's physical and psychological health. Symptoms and ill-effects may include loss of concentration, reduced performance, and frequent absence due to illness, which impacts the organization and puts the mobbed at fault. The organization ultimately finds grounds to terminate the employee or force the individual to resign. (Davenport et al., 1999). This practice continues unhampered, eliminating those who are not liked to feed the mobber's pleasure and hunger to control or reinforce prejudice. When the practice becomes an integral part of the organization's culture, it enters the realm of cultural norms—thus making it crucial that mobbing be identified immediately.

Escalatory, Sequential and Independent Aggression

While Einarsen (2004) described bullying as escalatory aggression. Glomb and Miner (2003) distinguished between escalatory (or sequential) aggression and independent aggression. The first form of aggression moves from a low-level, relatively minor, behavior to more severe aggressive and damaging behavior. The second form of aggression, which consists of more extreme behavior, does not arise from a lower level of behavior and may be associated with workplace violence. In either case, workers may become targets who run the risk of responding with reciprocal aggression (Robinson & O'Leary-Kelly, 1998). The assumption of mutuality in the escalatory process is consistent with the literature on escalated conflict, where at some point (regardless of who initiated the action) the conflict become increasingly reciprocated (Bodin, 1994).

Identifying Characteristics of Bully-Prone Workplace Environments

According to Leymann (1996), the workplace is the only remaining battlefield where people can run into each other without being taken into court. A state-wide Michigan survey in 2004 found that 14% of employees had experienced bullying and 56% had experienced occasional aggression (Keasley & Neuman, 2004). However, there are no laws prohibiting workplace bullying and unless taken more seriously, more people will be psychologically injured. The severity of this phenomenon is far worse than other behavior prohibited by law. Its distressing prevalence indicates a worsening trend affecting all in the workplace, victims and non-victims alike. This practice is not new, but its effect on the health and well-being of those victimized is gradually being reported. According to a Canadian survey, physical violence is usually reported from sources outside the workplace; in comparison, psychological violence is most often reported within the organization—which is believed to be due to the covert nature of bullying that has to be identified using detailed observation (Blackwood & Bentley, 2013).

Research conducted over the last two decades has linked a negative organizational climate with psychological stress. Additionally, the bully may destroy not only the victim, but also the victim's community and support system (Namie, 2003). Workplace bullying can also lead to tragic events (Carbo & Hughes, 2010). Examples of these events include (1) a report of two separate airline accidents that resulted from the flight crew's being afraid to question the pilot's decisions, and (2) life- threatening and life-ending mistakes in health care environments where stress and bullying interfere with medical practice (Carbo & Hughes, 2010).

The culture and climate of an organization tends to be consistent throughout all levels and are reflected in the behavior style of the director and senior management. In order for bullying to be established, it must occur within a culture that persists or even rewards this kind of behavior (Brodsky, 1976). When organizations are directive and authoritarian, people often feel their needs are being ignored. The bureaucratic structure can promote bullying since it involves those at the top with prerogative power who may have few interactions with those at the bottom. An injustice goes unchallenged for three reasons: first, people do not see the misuse of power; second, working people as well as managers believe that working people are incapable of supervising themselves and must have "leaders" who are inherently superior; and third, people lack the behavioral knowledge and skills necessary to envision collaborative organizations and make them function (Namie, 2003). The perception of a subordinate worker as inferior enhances the bullying process because it supports the claim that the victim is to blame and is therefore worthy of the treatment received.

Neuburger (1989) described potential risk factors for WP, such as the "micro-politics" of an organization, which refers to how an entity uses its formal/informal processes to achieve its business goals. When members of an organization do not fully understand these organizational processes, a power imbalance can occur, which increases the likelihood for WP (Mir, 2009). Similarly, Child (1972) noted that workplace bullying can be perpetuated by the organizational structure of a business—namely the formal allocation of work roles and the administrative mechanisms to control and integrate work activities. When such structures are poorly defined, it can lead to increased levels of role conflict and role ambiguity (Van Sell, Brief & Schuler, 1981).

Zapf and Einarsen (2003) point out that leaders may cause interpersonal conflict or aggression when their first priority is protecting their self-interests. "Tyrannical leadership behavior such as arbitrariness or belittling subordinates has not been studied explicitly, probably because ineffective leadership normally implies only the absence of those factors that make leadership ineffective" (Zapf et al., 1996, p. 216). However, recent approaches on studies of bullying have adopted an ecological perspective that examines the broader contexts in which bullying can occur (Namie & Namie, 2003). According to Matthiesen (2006), if leaders behave in a rude an insensitive way, it is more likely that subordinates will feel humiliated or subjected to bullying compared to interpersonal conflicts taking place between workers of equal position in the organizational hierarchy. Interpersonal hostility leads to high costs for organizations, in the form of increased absenteeism and higher turnover of personnel, decreased commitment and productivity, and negative publicity (e.g. Asforth, 1997; Hoel, Einarsen & Cooper, 2003; Tepper, 2000). The spill-over effects into society, includes lower productivity, early retirements, and increased health costs (Salin, 2005).

Important to this investigation is that bullying is widely practiced in governmental organizations, and particularly in the military (which will be detailed in a later section). Although these organizations typically have high job security, there often tends to be too few objective measures of performance. Moreover, there can frequent tension between loyalty to the institution and loyalty to the purpose of the organization. The nursing and social services fields often encounter this problem, which may help to explain why bullying in these fields is highly prevalent (Leymann, 1990b, 1993, 1996). According to Leymann (1990), personality factors are irrelevant as a cause of bullying; instead, work conditions are the primary cause. He further suggested four factors eliciting bullying behaviors in the work environment: (1) deficiencies in work design, (2) deficiencies in leadership behavior, (3) the victim's socially exposed position, (4) low department morale. Overall, however, according to Einarsen (2000), personality factors such as envy represent the core reason behind bullying.

O'Moore, Sergue, McGuire, Smith, & Seigne (1998) canvassed 30 Irish victims of bullying about the nature of their workplace, which they described as highly stressful and competitive. They further elaborated that the environment was unfriendly, plagued with interpersonal conflicts, unsupportive during times of organizational change, and managed by an authoritarian leadership style. Similarly, Zapf (1996) utilized cross-sectional studies in Germany to report that workplaces prone to WB were characterized by interpersonal conflicts and impair information flow.

According to Namie (2003), there are six types of organizations that are more likely to become bully-prone workplace. First, organizations that are pressured to "make the numbers" (i.e., respond to budget cuts) could inadvertently promote divisive relationships and create a climate of cut-throat competition and disrespect. Management in such workplaces may seek to eliminate employees by forcing them out through WB—and/or the victim reaches the breaking point. When this occurs the victim is often blamed for losing control, and too often management does not take the time to identify the cause of the outburst (Namie, 2002). Moreover, although others may witness the outburst and be privy to the reasons behind it, they may choose to remain silent because (a) they are in league with the bullier, or (b) they fear becoming victims on the job chopping-block themselves. Second, there may be organizations who reward people (i.e., move them up the managerial ladder) based on the strength of their personality or interpersonal aggressiveness while ignoring emotional intelligence. Problems develop when people are placed in managerial and supervisory positions without accounting for their ability or willingness to be objective in evaluating subordinates. Even though supervisory managers may possess high technical skills and be well liked, they are not immune from becoming bullies (Namie, 2003).

Third, organizations with only short-term plans may become bully-prone. Short-term planning that results in failing to meet stakeholder expectations is likely to create problems of finger-pointing and blame—and thus the possibility of bullying (Namie, 2003). Fourth, organizations may become susceptible to bullying if their internal conduct codes do not establish ethical rules of conduct that govern the organization, as well as inculcate methods addressing bullying. When bullying is not expressly prohibited in these codes, the practice remains tolerated. Such organizations need to broaden their prohibitions to incidents such as bullying and establish these practices as unacceptable (Hoag, 2004). Fifth, in some bully-prone organizations, executives accord higher priority to personal friendships than legitimate business interests (Namie, 2003). In other words, when a bully has management's favor and faces no accountability due to their actions, other workers become irritated—knowing that if they seek legal redress management will do nothing. Moreover, Namie (2003) asserted that targets feel that will not be promoted regardless how well they perform since management has become an accomplice of the bully, "…either deliberately or inadvertently by allowing it to continue unabated" (Namie, 2003, p.11). Sixth and most importantly, a bully-prone organization only exists in an environment of fear—e.g., employees fear losing their jobs because they are insecure in having to constantly "make numbers." Furthermore, fear is engineered either deliberately or unintentionally when work requirements change constantly because there is no long-range planning (Namie, 2003).

Other researchers have also addressed the types of organizations that either promote bullying or turn a blind eye to it. Ruthless cost- cuttings and mergers have caused whole layers of management to instantly disappear, affecting those in lower levels of the organization who may feel they have to dance to the tune of top management in order to stay employed—regardless of their demands (Field, 1996).

The Response of Management in Bully-Prone Workplaces

Usually when management is confronted with punishing a bully, it either denies the allegation (the first line of defense) or lightly punishes the bully when the problem can no longer be denied. In fact, entire groups may remain in denial if they are unwilling to change group behavior. Most often, management denies the abuse because three popular beliefs are threatened (Adams, 1992): (1) people operate as independent individuals and are not controlled by group behavior; (2) behavior is under continuous rational control; and (3) workplaces have people's interests at heart. Management chooses to adhere to this third belief even though in actuality, they may not. Norms establish denial in order to prevent change and ensure that the values of the group remain intact. If members of the group contest the norms, they face rejection from the group and ultimately may become victims themselves (Smart & Leary, 2009). Norms are also enforced by the "norm of silence," which prevents members of the group from speaking out about change. The norm of silence establishes a homeostatic rule that makes discussing problems a taboo. Because there is silence, people in the culture will either not hear you, resist you, misunderstand you, or feel attacked if you attempt to draw their attention to a perceived injustice—thereby perpetuating institutional norms (Adams, 1992). In addition to resorting to denials, organizations may purposefully fail to resolve conflicts and resort to scapegoating. The employee may be punished without due process, conflicts remain unresolved, and the boss avoids undue scrutiny and possible vilification by workers if found to be in error (Namie, 2003).

It must be noted, however, that the presence of norms does not necessarily negate organizational values. Organizations may hold values that contradict practices and these values are not always negative. Organizations may also have positive norms that support the health of the organization. The question may arise: "Why do people adopt organizational norms?" One reason is that people generally operate best when their behavior is congruent with the group and they are not being distracted by internal struggles and anxieties. They, therefore, block out the interruptions, which also helps to reduce stress. People often adopt norms because they depend on feedback from others who provide positive confirmation of their self-esteem (Adams, 1992). According to Adams (1992) in adopting organizational norms, several steps must be followed. First, an individual begins to see the world through the reality of the new beliefs, aided by necessary rationalizations that still are being constructed; the individual recognizes the need to conform. Second, the individual sees the norms as a reality and conformance enforces it. Third, people blame themselves for any remaining stress/discomfort due to having to do it "their way" and as a result use norm enforcement.

Many co-workers may also fail to support victims due to such phenomena as the 'Abilene Paradox," "Group Think" and "Cognitive Dissonance"

(Festinger, 1957; see also Janis, 1972; Harvey 1996). The Abilene Paradox occurs when people imagine the worst possible outcomes if they violate group norms that reinforce compliance (Adams, 1992). According to Harvey (1996), the Abilene Paradox refers to circumstances in which the limit of a particular situation seems to force a group of people to act in a way contrary to what they actually want. This situation can occur when groups continue with misguided activities—which no group member desires, but nor is he or she willing to raise objections or displease the others.

Similarly, Group Think describes how members of a group are incapable of critically assessing the pros and cons of their decisions. The group members are cohesive and prefer to remain united and ignore any nagging doubts. Adams (1992) pointed out that in Group Think, members are easily led by a forceful leader and align themselves with that person to stay in good favor. Adams further noted that Group Think carries with it a code of silence that conforms to a bully's strategy. Witnesses to the contrary are squelched because group members rationalize the conflict or deny negative effects in order to maintain feelings of self-satisfaction.

The third factor associated with failing to support one or more victims of bullying is known as Cognitive Dissonance (CD), which has also been called "the mind controller's best friend" (Levine, 2003, p. 202). CD asserts that human beings feel it is psychologically uncomfortable to hold contradictory opinions; thus, in order to avoid CD, a person will try to maintain their cognition, attitude, or behavior (Levine, 2003).

Bully and Social Undermining

According to Vinokur and Van Ryan (1993), bullying behaviors can induce "social undermining," which refers to direct or indirect negative interaction that disrupts one's social network and causes a considerable amount of stress (Duffy, Gangster & Pagan, 2002). Vinokur and Van Ryan (1993) synthesized early studies of social conflict to develop their definition of social undermining. Related behaviors include acts directed toward a target that indicate or display:

(a) negative affect (anger, dislike), (b) negative evaluation of the target in terms of his or her attributes, actions, and efforts (criticism), and /or (c) "actions that hinder the attainment of instrumental goals" (Vinokur, Price & Caplan, 1996, p. 167).

Social undermining caused by insidious indirect bullying gradually weakens a victim. Tactics include the "silent treatment" (i.e., ignoring the presence of a target) or refusing to provide resources needed to perform tasks— either of which can cause harm and diminish a target's ability to establish and maintain a positive self-image. "Two distinct sources of social undermining are supervisors and co-workers since these are likely to be the most important functional and social constituencies in an organization" (Duffy et al., 2002, p. 331). Duffy et al. (2002) added that "social undermining may take the form of direct actions, such as intentionally saying derogatory things about a person, rejecting someone outright, or belittling someone's ideas" (p. 335). According to Baron and Neuman (1997), other undermining tactics include withholding information and failing to defend someone against negative attacks. An example of social undermining would be an individual withholding praise from a target in order to weaken his or her standing in the organization, to minimize goal accomplishment, or to draw the attention of supervisors away from the target (Duffy et al., 2002).

Social undermining may cause aggression and employee deviance; the latter refers to behavior that violates institutionalized expectations or norms and, in doing so, threatens the well-being of an organization and its members (O'Leary-Kelly, Duffy, & Griffin, 2000). Deviance, however, is a much broader concept than social undermining and can be both organizational and interpersonal. Deviant behaviors can include minor actions such as gossiping or showing favoritism to actual physical assault (Duffy et al., 2002). Greenberg and Scott (1996) identified two form of employee deviance: production and property deviance. Production deviance is behavior that violates formally established norms in the organization in connection with the quality and quantity of work to be accomplished on one's job (Publich & Tornigny, 2004). Property damage occurs when an employee damages or acquires tangible assets without authorization (Everton, Jolton, & Mastrangel, 2007). An example of property damage would include an employee making intentional errors or committing theft.

Aspects of Social Support

According to Gangster and Pagan (2002) the converse of social undermining is social support. Coworkers provide social support to the victim by refusing to follow the bully's pattern of ostracism and rejection. They reinforce the victim's self-worth, reduce his/her feelings of isolation, and help moderate the negative aspects of a toxic work environment (Lewis & Oxford, 2005). Zapf et al. (1996) found that higher levels of social support from supervisors were associated with lower levels of criticism and threat, and greater support from colleagues. Despite the benefits of social support, victims who are particularly distressed may have difficulty accepting support from others because they may have developed inappropriate attitudes toward others. According to Einarsen (2002), victims who are highly distressed may display behaviors thought to be inappropriate within a work context. Often the strategies they use to reduce the amount of their stress further increases it and they may get caught in a cycle of stress which causes them to make poor decisions (WBI, 2012).

Under the influence of roles, social networks and status, social structures can affect one's health, values, occupational attainment, and sense of belonging in society. This is a primary reason social support and social networks are so important to individuals. They may ward off stressful situations that negatively impact a person's life. An individual experiencing social disintegration may benefit from both informal and formal social support and networks. According to Mikkelson (1995) social support and social networks are helpful because: Individuals share health information that helps them identify sources of health problems; friendship networks promote a sense of responsibility toward others, which may cause members to take greater responsibility for members who feel bullied. Einarsen (2002) further suggested that a group's capacity to communicate, coordinate, and control should increase the flow of support to its members because:

- Individuals share health information that helps them identify sources of health problems; friendship networks promote a sense of responsibility toward others, which may cause members to take greater responsibility for members who feel that it makes a difference whether they live or die;
- Support systems may mitigate psychological stress; and
- The presence of others reduces anxiety and may mitigate the development of health and/or psychological problems.

In a bully-prone workplace, a collective consciousness arises among organizational members that often excludes the target. Lewis and Orford (2005) investigated this theory by conducting a qualitative study looking at the subjective experiences of ten women targets of workplace bullying. They reported that "lack of support signifies a decrease in a targets' resources and ability to defend themselves, increases their vulnerability to the bully and shifts the imbalance of power further towards the bully" (p. 42). In short, their results confirmed that complex social processes are involved in the evolution and perpetuation of workplace bullying.

According to Einarsen et al. (1994) there is a positive relationship between workplace bullying and social support from supervisors and colleagues. However, research seems to indicate that there are institutional barriers that make such support a challenge—and that there may be some gender differences. "In terms of power holding and social support, it seems likely that women and men may differ in these experiences and perceptions of the processes involved in workplace bullying, but this remains unclear" (Lewis & Orford, 2005, p. 31). To attempt to clarify this ambiguity, Lewis and Orford (2005) conducted a qualitative study whose primary purpose was to examine the perceptions of workplace bullying among women targets and how they felt they were influenced by the dynamics of social relations. A second purpose for this study was to gather information to help organizations and individuals develop a better understanding of workplace bullying, thus facilitating more effective responses and coping mechanisms. Ten volunteers (all targets of bullying) were selected from two groups: Sample A and Sample B. Volunteers from Sample A were recruited from a National UK voluntary helpline. Volunteers from Sample B were recruited by via personal contacts. All volunteer's ages were in their 30s to 50s, married, and held professional occupations in the public sector.

Grounded theory provided the methodological foundation for this study, since its intent is to investigate phenomena of interest that is rooted or grounded in observation (Charmaz, 1995; Trochim, Marcus, Weld, Masse, & Richard, 2008). Using semi-structured interviews, the authors explored how targets of workplace bullying perceived bullying behaviors and how they sought, accessed and received social support. A detailed analysis of results indicated that participants experienced diminished support from colleagues in the workplace once they recognized any potential risks they might encounter by supporting the victim. As a result, at best they only gave covert and passive support to them. Thus, victims began to fear disclosing information about bullies to colleagues for fear of it getting back to the source of the bullying. They also did not adequate receive support from those in responsible management and trade union positions, which increased barriers to institutional support. Specifically, the authors noted: "Union officials were committed to maintaining union funds and their own career advancement, and avoided conflict with management; for managers, recognition of bullying was personally and organizationally threatening, raising questions of responsibility and challenging management competence" (p. 39). Participants observed certain patterns of responses from management and trade unions when seeking support; most of the women agreed that management tried to shift the focus the women by "personalizing the problem." Such a strategy effectively kept management and union officials from really understanding the nature of the bullying. "Being heard refers to qualities of others listening and responses to participants' disclosures of problems at work" (Lewis & Orford, 2005, p. 36). Interestingly, Participants received support from others—but primarily outside of the workplace. Nonetheless, they all reported the support to be extremely helpful in supporting their self-worth, maintaining some degree of stability on the job, and eliminating self-blame (Peterson, Maier, & Seligman, 1995).

As an indication of the negative spin-off effects of WB, Oxford & Lewis (2005) also discussed how stresses created in the workplace can extend beyond the office. This "ripple effect" also tended to diminish the degree of social support the participants received at home. "Personal relationships were seen as best surviving and even relationships which participants had experienced as strong and supportive were unable to work well as bullying continued" (Lewis & Orford, 2005, p. 36). Participants reported having problems of anxiety, diminished self-esteem and a threatened sense of self—emphasizing that their distress was due to the breakdown of roles and relationships at home and work. "Personal relationships and key roles were damaged through bullying and maintaining beliefs in self and the world became more difficult" (Lewis & Orford, 2005, p. 40).

A number of scholars (e.g., Zapf & Einarsen, 2001) have asserted that workplace bullying is a complex and evolving social process, which is very much impacted by the presence or absence of social support. Moreover, when victims are misguidedly directed by management to look within themselves for the source of the bullying, it "…reduced the availability of support, and may have impeded the processes of recognition and disclosure by targets who blamed themselves for the difficulties they experienced (maintaining self)" (Lewis & Orford, 2005, p. 41). Lewis and Orford (2005) suggested that "blaming the victim" is all too common in cases of WB, which not only enables the bullying to remain an invisible problem—but may have the unintended effect of allowing the bullying to escalate. In contrast, when responsible parties in the organization and union officials have intervened, the situations for targets have greatly improved. A practical issue in drawing intervention is the gathering of evidence to support claims of the victims (Zapf & Gross, 2001). This "naming" process—i.e., identifying the experience for what it really was—became important to maintaining self (Lewis & Orford, 2005).

In a similar study involving gender differences, Lewis (2006) conducted a qualitative research study with 10 White, British, female participants, aged 40-59, who had identified themselves as targets of workplace bullying. All were university educated and were public-sector professionals. Lewis explored the frequency, forms and effects of workplace bullying among women, since previous studies have shown they differ from those of men (Rayner & Cooper, 1997). For example, Archer (1999) found bullying to be an accepted cultural component in the white male cultural component among fire fighters. After synthesizing the interview data, Lewis (2006) found five major strategies targets used to recognize and cope with workplace bullying: (1) minimizing interpersonal difficulties, (2) preserving self, (3) monitoring commitments to professional and organizational values and cultures, (4) sickness explanations, and (5) naming the problem. "These were not linear or sequential processes, but ongoing and complex responses to changing circumstances, in particular given that bullying appeared to escalate overtime" (Lewis, 2006, p. 125). Participants minimized difficult interpersonal behaviors, which tended to be subtle, ambiguous and directed at individual targets, as trivial at first. In fact, the participants did not initially view these acts as bullying—it was only in retrospect that they recognized a pattern of bullying. Once it became known for what it was, however, "All participants … reflected on, and identified contradictions between values underlying professional practices towards services users and values underlying management practice toward themselves" (Lewis, p. 126). These contradictions caused participants to lose trust in their organizations.

Naming the problem was difficult because the participants could not make sense of changed experiences. They also could not predict that trivial behaviors would escalate—but when they did the participants developed a state of shock. One woman who DID confront the issue squarely was more effective in coping with her situation. "Naming her experiences as bullying was the start of her recovery and impacted her sense of self" (Lewis, 2006, p 128). All participants indicated that the bullying experiences affected their physical and/or mental health. Although health care professionals later validated their problems, they had not initially recognized these problems as arising from WB. Thus, a corollary finding of this study is that health care professionals need increased awareness of the symptoms of bullying to identify the negative impacts on the victim's psychological and physical health.

Negative Impacts of Workplace Bullying

Although single acts of aggression and harassment do occur fairly often in everyday interactions, when they occur on a regular basis they can jeopardize a victim's mental and physical health and well-being (Einarsen & Raknes, 1997; Leymann, 1987). The covert nature of workplace bullying can destroy a target's health and ability to work, and thus can result in secondary impacts to financial security (Fisher-Blando, 2008). Victims of bullying at work have also been shown to have low self-esteem and to be anxious in social settings (Einarsen et al., 1994).

Vartia-Vaananen (2003) described the association between exposure to bullying and increased levels of psychological complaints, depression, burnout anxiety, aggression, and psychosomatic and musculoskeletal health complaints—in other words, similar to symptoms of Post-Traumatic Stress Disorder (PTSD). Subsequent studies have also addressed the detrimental effects of bullying and non-sexual harassment in the workplace on employee health and well-being (Dubois, Faley, Kustis, & Knapp, 1999; Einarsen, 1999; Einarsen et al., 2003; Hoel et al., 1999).

Workplace bullies can exert serious negative impacts upon their victims (Namie & Namie, 2003; Prentice, 2005), in addition to damage to institutional morale and productivity. Brodsky (1996) identified three patterns of effects on victims. They are:

- Vague physical symptoms such as weakness, loss of strength, chronic fatigue, aches and pains;
- Depression and related symptoms such as impotence, lack of self-esteem and sleeplessness; and
- Psychological symptoms such as hostility, hypersensitivity, memory

problems, feelings of victimization, nervousness, and avoidance of social contact.

Effects on Physical Health

Most physical health symptoms resulting from bullying are slow to be unidentified since they mimic symptoms that result from other sources. Nonetheless, these symptoms require immediate attention from health professionals and others concerned with the health and well-being of employees. Symptoms seen most often are stress-related, including tearfulness, headaches, colds, coughs, sullenness indicative of psychological hurt, susceptibility to illnesses such as minor infections, flu-like symptoms and aches and pains (Field, 1996). Of particular concern for deleterious health outcomes is the impact of the "screaming mimi bully," who controls victims through fear that they will launch at the target at anytime (Namie & Namie, 2000) via scolding or unprovoked harsh judgments. When the victim attempts to ignore or avoid this behavior, the bully becomes even more aggressive. Victims of the screaming mimi have reported stomach problems, headaches, back spasms, and skin reactions, among others. The symptoms tend to increase with the duration of exposure to the bullying (Namie & Namie, 2000).

Workplace bullying—and particularly its extreme form, mobbing—can cause severe illnesses, psychological distress, occupational/financial hardship, social exclusion and even suicide. It frequently generates chronic syndromes of combined psycho-physical disorders, restricting and impairing the affected person. After a relatively short period of time the victim can also develop General Anxiety Disorder (GAD). At this stage, severe depression and/or obsessive syndrome may develop, irreversibly altering the personality of the affected person (Groeblinghoff & Becker, 1996). Indeed, a healthy and competent employee can be driven to economic, physical, and emotional ruin within a matter of a few weeks or months simply as a result of WP—if management fails to intervene in any proactive way. To reiterate, the corollary damage from WP is wide-ranging and can include one or more of the following physical ailments (Namie & Namie, 2000):

- Reduced immunity to infections: more colds, flu
- Itching skin disorders
- Stress headaches
- Increased allergies, asthma
- Indigestion, colitis, irritable bowel syndrome
- Rheumatoid arthritis, fibromyalgia
- Hair loss
- Weight swings
- Hypertension
- Diabetes mellitus
- Peptic ulcers
- Heart attack

Effects on Psychological Health

Field (1996) described a range of psychological symptoms associated with WP: overwhelming negativism, obsessiveness with the situation, irrational inability to be associated with or touch or handle material associated with the situation, an overwhelming urge to talk about what's going on, hypersensitivity to criticism or implied criticism or remarks, hypervigilance, poor concentration, mood swings, wavering objectivity, increased self-deprecation and self-effacement. Victim are also prone "apologize for existing" and be fixated on doing something proactive about bullying (p. 127). Researchers have has identified bullying as being associated with cognitive deficits such as concentration problems, insecurity and lack of initiative (Leyman, 1992; O'Moore et al., 1998). These problems are almost inevitably linked to negative impacts on organizational productivity due to reduced levels of motivation, creativity, and a rise in accidents and mistakes (Einarsen, Hoel, Dieter, Zapf & Cooper, 2003). Moreover, when a victim's private life is also attached, results shown the strongest psychological correlation between bullying and psychological ill health (Zapf et al., 1996). Horstein (1996) added that there is a statistically-significant correlation between disrespect, depression and the loss of self-esteem.

Victims of bullying may suffer from hyper-vigilance or paranoia (Field, 1996). The former is a feature of PTSD and seems to stem from a combination of distrust, obsession, fear, anxiety, and alarm. Relations with one's partner are also at risk. Persons suffering from paranoia believe that someone is actively pursuing them. Their experiences differ from people experiencing hypervigilance (i.e., being on high alert for a range of problems) in that the paranoid victim is mistrustful of everyone, and if not treated, is likely to have a breakdown requiring professional help (Field, 1996). In essence, the later stages of hypervigilance may lead to paranoia. Victims of either exhibit withdrawal and are reluctant to communicate for fear of further criticism from the perpetrator. As a result of this injury, the victim can develop a dependence on alcohol or other substances leading to impoverished performance, poor concentration and failing memory. Risks of accidents also increase.

Mental breakdowns can occur due to tremendous negative stress, which creates demands beyond the capacity of the brain to process. These demands are usually unreasonable, unwarranted, unnecessary and unacceptable (Field, 1996), making the identification of a tenable solution almost impossible. "If the two minds [the conscious and the unconscious] become trapped in a loop, with the conscious mind seeking, with increasing desperation, a solution, it is only possible to break out of this never-ending cycle by (a) the injection of new information or insight, (b) outside intervention, or (c) an external or intrusive event of sufficient magnitude" (Field, 1996, p. 132). Field added that a major problem could arise when the subconscious mind devises bizarre solutions to unsolvable problems, which further increases the disrespect and attacks from the bully.

Griffiths (1981) described stress as being driven beyond one's coping abilities and beyond one's capacity to function effectively, while the AARP Bulletin (2010) defined job strain as a form of psychological stress resulting from having demanding jobs that do not allow decision-making or the exercise of creativity. Stress is real. More than three-quarters of American workers (78%) describe their jobs as stressful and 75-90% of visits to primary care physicians are for stress-related problems, and up to 80% of on-the-job accidents are stress related (Upstate Medical University, 2010). According to Quick, Cooper, Quick, and Gavin (2002), the costs to US organizations for stress-related absenteeism and illnesses is approximately $150 billion per year. The AARP Bulletin (2010) linked job stress to high blood pressure and the likelihood of cardiovascular disease.

Stress occurs in three stages and usually begins with an alarm to the body's defense system. This triggers the "fight or flight" response—namely, the sympathetic nervous system releases adrenalin to deal with the stress (Namie & Namie, 2000). Resistance to stress begins in the second stage at which point the body can resume normal functioning. In the case of WP, however, since the bullying may be continuous the body's defense system may become depleted (Namie & Namie, 2000). In the third and final stage of stress, the victim may experience a full system breakdown, both mentally and physically. This only occurs after all warning signs from the body have been ignored. If the stressor is not removed it can eventually claim the victim's life.

Bullying and Post Traumatic Stress Disorder. As noted earlier, the effects of bullying have been likened to PTSD, which according to Randall (1997) include the following core symptoms:

- Feelings and actions associated with beliefs of experiencing stressful events;
- Intense psychological stress occurring when exposed to events associated with the trauma;
- Nightmares, difficulty sleeping, incontinence, poor concentration, irritability, and other psychological arousals when exposed to stimuli reminiscent of the trauma;
- Aggressive behavior problems;
- Moodiness; and
- Feelings of guilt

Bullying and Prolonged Duress Stress Disorder. People who are traumatized at work can also suffer from the symptoms of Prolonged Duress Stress Disorder (PDSD) (Scott & Strandling, 1994), which results from the cumulative experiences of a series of bullying events rather than a single event. Targets are assaulted over a long period of time, with no single episode seemingly harsh enough to disrupt the target's life. With PDSD, certain types of events initiate "triggers" that may be unrecognized, but nonetheless set off certain reactions that may be violent or passive-aggressive, immediate or delayed, which resemble symptoms of PTSD. The difference is that there is no specific trauma as is needed for a PTSD diagnosis. On the basis of case studies, Scott and Strandling (1994) asserted that enduring psychological stress may produce symptoms of PTSD.

Effects on Self-Esteem

Self-esteem corresponds to an individual's self-evaluation and beliefs about his/her potency or efficacy, ability and worth (Harvey, 1996). Workers subjected to bullying in the form of abuse, disrespect, and belittling are at risk for diminished self-esteem (Harvey, 1996). Bullies may use intimidation to erode a subordinate's faith in themselves (Harvey, 1996). "Intimidated workers relinquish autonomy and work hard to avoid being hit by their bosses. Others forego self-direction in favor of self-protection" (p.79). Betrayal tactics may also be used to further undermine a worker's sense of self-worth (Horstein, 1996). Once an individual has lost self-confidence, the process of rebuilding it is a long and painful process even with professional help.

Although self-esteem is not factored into an organization's profit-and-loss statements, bullying-related hits to a worker's self-worth do negatively impact the organization. "Bosses who degrade their subordinates rob both the workers and their organization of valuable assets" (Horstein, 1996, p. 79). Individuals with low self-esteem experience self-doubt, anxiety, self-contempt, and ultimately depression (Beck, Ruch, Shaw & Emery, 1979). These individuals, however, are rarely aggressive because they are being subdued by the bully (Zapf & Einarsen, 2003).

Effects on Interpersonal Relationships

Einarsen (1996) and Zapf (1999) asserted that organizational and work conditions are environmental factors that can give rise to interpersonal conflicts, which are likely to escalate into bullying when values and norms within the organizational culture permit hostile work behavior. "Decades of psychological and psychiatric research evidence have confirmed everyday experience and common sense by demonstrating that individual well-being is affected by the quality of social interaction at work" (Horstein, 1996, p. 74).

Bandura (1977) suggested that employees usually adapt their behaviors to what they perceive as acceptable for the environment. For example, a person who is not naturally aggressive is nonetheless more likely to display aggressive behaviors when they are modeled in an organization. The "Attrition Model" proposed by Schneider (1975) suggested that those who display aggressive behaviors in a work group are retained by its members if their work group is aggressive—thereby preserving a relatively homogeneous work group. According to Glomb & Lisa (2003) two forms of aggression arises from work groups. A victim may be in a work group where people merely behave aggressively. This can be described as "ambient aggression." A victim may also be in a work group where the aggression is directed solely toward the victim. Glomb and Lisa (2003) described this scenario as "discretionary aggression," which veers into the real of WB.

Effects on Job Satisfaction and Career

Workplace bullying negatively impacts individual job satisfaction and performance. Schat and Frone (2011) suggested that there are two forms of job performance—task performance and contextual performance. "Task performance involves behaviors that fulfill the prescribed duties of a given job and contextual performance (also referred to as organizational leadership) involves behaviors that contribute to the maintenance and enhancement of the social-psychological work environment (p. 23). Research shows that abusive supervision is a known predictor for reduced contextual performance

(Aryee, Chen, Sun & Deborah, 2007). Similarly, Harris, Kaemar, & Zivnuska (2007) found that while abusive supervisory practices tend to be unrelated to supervisor-ratings, they are negatively related to supervisor ratings of tasks performance and to formal performance appraisal ratings of the supervisee (i.e., the victim).

Interestingly, the stresses associated with workplace aggression can serve to motivate an individual either positively or negatively (Cavanaugh, Boswell, Roehling & Boudreau (2000). The former, which are known as challenge stressors, can increase motivation by leading to feelings of challenge and achievement. The latter—namely, hindrance stressors—negatively impact individual motivation and performance goals (Cavanaugh et al, 2000). Schat and Frone (2011) suggest that those exposed to workplace aggression with a hindrance stressor are more likely to suffer from lower motivation, a diminished work capacity, and negative work attitudes. Additionally, such stressors are known to diminish an individual's health and well-being (Schat & Frone, 2011).

Researchers have found a relatively strong negative association between exposure to bullying and lowered job satisfaction and commitment (Hoel & Cooper, 2000a; Keashly & Jagatic, 2000; Price & Spratlen 1995; Quince, 1999). Behaviors used by the bully to humiliate, intimidate, frighten or punish the victim can cause them to become unable to cope with daily tasks and meet the requirements of the job (Einarsen, 2000). Job satisfaction is negatively impacted as the target's productivity decreases and costly mistakes occur due to persistent antagonism. The bully can cause a victim to hate his/her job and dread even going to work. A job once loved becomes a source of depression or triggers thoughts of a career change. Frustration may even carry over into the victim's family life (Namie & Namie, 2000).

Field (1996) asserted that a person who has been bullied out of their job by a vicious and vindictive person has no desire to quit their job—rather they only want to get back to work and continue the career of their choice. However, an older worker, in particular, may be forced out to an "early retirement" due to WB, thereby risking a cut in pension benefits.. A younger worker may have to accept a lesser-paying job or go on unemployment benefits, which can be a frustrating experience. In fact, depending on state laws, an individual may be ineligible for unemployment benefits if the individual has "voluntarily" resigned. Consider, too, the loss of health care benefits for those who leave work due to WB; thus conceivably negating the possibility of obtaining mental health counseling and treatment. If the victim applies for worker's compensation benefits based on having become partially or fully incapacitated due to psychological injury or stress-related illnesses, he or she may not be covered in some states. As Yamada (2003) noted, an individual seeking social security benefits due to bullying must establish that he/she left voluntarily due to intolerable conditions, which is challenging at best.

Effects on Organizational Productivity

Any attempt to assess the productivity costs (and thus the financial impact) of workplace bullying is difficult because there are many questions about quality of data and reliable connections between cause and effect Hoel & al. (2001). The effects of bullying are reflected in several outcomes. Harbison (2004) stated that absenteeism is the most common result of WB. He estimated that a company of 1000 employees loses $720,000 per year due to employee absenteeism. Sheehan, Bucker, and Rayner (1999) cited a range of outcomes of bullying: 83% staff turnover, 87% reduced efficiency, and a 19-28% decline in the quality of work. The researchers also indicated that 18% of workers worldwide sought counseling as a result of bullying, 10% required mediation, 10% had increased error rates, 5% reported unsafe workplaces, 3% lodged workers' compensation claims, 2% took anti-discrimination action, and 1% took other actions.

On-the-job accidents can also result from stress-related WB. Worker compensation claims in the U.S. from job stress are estimated to cost $200 to $300 billion annually as assessed by absenteeism, diminished productivity, employee turnover, accidents, direct medical legal and insurance fees, worker's compensation award, etc. Another study estimates that 40% of worker turnover is due to job stress, while also reporting that compensation claims related to job stress in California have skyrocketed anywhere from 60-80%, thus costing employers almost $1.6 billion in medical and legal fees (Namie & Namie, 2003). Seago (1996) further noted that the unpredictability and unexpectedness of unscheduled absenteeism interferes with the normal operation of the organization and, where applicable, the quality of services provided.

According to Field (1996), the consequences of WB for the employer are varied and serious:

- Low productivity
- Increase in mistakes due to poor concentration and lack of attention to detail (see also Leymann, 1992; O'Moore, Sergue, McGuire, & Smith, 1998)
- Unwillingness of victims to follow procedures
- Reduced quality
- Low morale
- Absenteeism (see also Steer & Rhodes, 1978)
- High staff turnover
- Unexplained absences during normal working hours
- Impoverished interpersonal skills and relations between and with customers, colleagues, peers, subordinates, suppliers, contractors, self-contractors, authorities, regulatory bodies, professional bodies, etc.,
- Employees spending more and more time protecting themselves and less and less time on real work.

A 1990 study by the American Bureau of National Affairs (as reported by Randall, 1997) indicated that between $5-6 billion are lost each year due to decreased productivity resulting from actual or perceived employee abuse. Farrell (2002) pointed to another study that shows 82% of people targeted by bullies leave their workplace: 38% for health reasons and 44% because of performance reviews manipulated to show them as incompetent. The organization's replacement costs for these employees usually far exceeds their salaries. Similarly, Steer and Rhodes (1978) reported that WB leads to employee absenteeism, supporting the relationship between bullying and ill health. Einarsen (2003), in fact, asserted that "increased health problems associated with perceived bullying may also demotivate individuals to attend through reduced job satisfaction due to bullying" (p 148).

Zapf & Gross (2001) revealed that frequent sick absenteeisms seemed to help victims cope more successfully with bullying. However, the implicit and explicit pressure to go to work can be so strictly enforced that it may be considered an act of bullying in its own right (UNISON, 1997). Sinclair, Ironside, and Seifect (1996) referred to this coercion as a disciplinary effect—especially if the individual is reminded his or her absence puts a strain on coworkers. Another disciplinary effect is linking absenteeism with the possibility of job loss, for example, in connection with downsizing of the organization (Voss, Fiderus, & Dideruhsen, 2001). Workers who fear making a mistake or drawing attention to themselves "... may also affect their relationships with co-workers and supervisors, possibly sharpening rather than reducing the conflict, which again will impact on the total productivity of the work unit" (Einarsen, 2003, p. 151).

Organizational productivity can also be stifled as a result of complaints and grievances brought by victims who have perceived being bullied. Resulting investigations are time-consuming and often are a tremendous drain on organizational resources. In California, compensation for wrongful termination of contracts have been reported to average up to $400,000, excluding the cost to employers for out-of-court settlements (Wilson, 1991). If no clear policies and procedures are in place, litigations can last for years (Einarsen et al., 1994). A typical outcome of these litigations is the permanent separation of the perpetrator and the victim. Unfortunately, evidence shows the victim is usually transferred (Raynor, Hoel, and Cooper, 2002). As noted, however, organizations suffer as a result of transfers with costs for replacement and training (Dalton, 1997).

Finally, even more damaging to the organization than financial costs is the reputation it can gain as being a hostile workplace. In such instances recruitment becomes difficult, which may lead to skill shortages (Glendinning, 2001). Being accused of bullying—rightly or wrongly—is still likely to affect both the accused and the organization. Even if cases are resolved satisfactorily, there may still be a tremendous price to pay in terms of organizational upheaval and damage to the organizational brand or reputation (Hoel & Cooper, 2000b).

Effects of Bullying on Bystanders and Witnesses

Adding to the collateral damage of workplace bullying are the lasting negative effects on colleagues/observers who have witnessed it (Vartia, 2001). The effects of bullying on bystanders or observers may be either direct or indirect. An example of a direct affect would be fear of becoming the next target. An indirect affect would include an employee feeling that their general well-being was reduced as a result of working in a hostile environment (Einarsen, 2002). Witnesses of bullying may suffer due to a real or perceived inability to help the target; in fact, studies show that more than one-third of witnesses of bullying reported that they wanted to help the target, but did not (Einarsen, 2002; Rayner, 1999). Moreover, when coworkers actually did step up to help, their strategies were usually ineffective (Rayner, 1998; 1999), which included confronting the bully, complaining to the bully's boss, complaining to personnel, and enlisting help from other colleagues. In fact, Rayner (1999) reported that 41% of respondents indicated that their efforts were ineffective. Many reported that they were labeled as troublemakers and 25% of the victims were reported as having been threatened with dismissal after they complained to management (Einarsen, 2002).

A study among municipal workers in Finland revealed that witnesses of workplace bullying reported more mental stress reactions that workers who had not witnessed bullying (Vartia, 2001). Interesting, in a study of 2,215 employees in Norway, 14% of workers perceived bullying as a daily strain; 21% of the employees reported lowered job satisfaction; and 27% claimed that bullying reduced their productivity—however, only 9.6% of the respondents claimed they had actually been bullied (Einarsen et al., 1994).

Organizational Culture and Workplace Bullying

Organizational culture is the personality of an organization formed by four components: assumptions, values, norms, and tangible signs. Members of a well-functioning organization tend to agree on what these components mean, while those not sharing them are regarded as outsiders (Klein, Masi, & Weidner II, 1995). Similarly, Schein (1993) defined organizational culture as a set of shared basic assumptions that one group learned as it is solved problems of external adaptation and internal integration—and that has worked well enough to be considered valid and therefore to be taught to new members as the correct way to perceive, think, and fell in relation to their problems. Culture, therefore, is deeply rooted in an organization's history and collective experience (Schein, 1993). It follows, then, that culture develops with stable membership and shared learning experiences. Organizations experiencing considerable turnover of members and leaders lack stability and shared assumptions needed to develop a culture (Schein, 2004).

In many cases, the organizational culture is culpable for the genesis and spread of workplace bullying when it fails to inculcate a culture that is understood by all to be intolerant of such behaviors. While it is true that the covert nature of WB helps to conceal and preserve its presence, every member of the organization should be encouraged to expose it for what it is. Unfortunately, although witnesses may understand what is happening, the particular culture of their organization may inhibit them from acting accordingly. Moreover, in such a culture the bully is likely to know that the organization may be reluctant to admit to bullying and thus feels secure in his/her role due to tacit organizational support.

The impact of organizational culture on the behavior and beliefs of workers cannot be overstated. According to Chao, Koylowski, Smith and Hedlund (1993), culture is everywhere. It affects an employee's morale, commitment, productivity, physical health, and emotional wellbeing. Empirical research has produced an impressive array of findings, demonstrating the importance of culture to enhancing organizational performance (e.g., Cameron & Ettington,

1988; Denison, 1990), several of which confront the insidiousness of workplace bullying.

Preventing and Addressing Bullying Behaviors

Organizations need to resolve conflicts as they occur, and employees must feel free to point out instances of WB regardless of the identity of the bully or power structure of the workplace (Adams, 1992). To facilitate this goal, the employer should (a) make clear organizational guidelines and ethical codes of behavior that promote the health and wellbeing of the workplace, (b) promote a sense of professionalism at all levels of the organization, (c) promote a climate of tolerance and freedom for various attitudes, and (d) refuse to sanction improper behavior (Cooper et al., 2000). The code of silence needs to be broken. The use of mediation and impartial third parties may be considered; however, many consultants feel mediation is not the way to deal with workplace bullying in that it ignores structural deficiencies within the organization. Additionally, organizations need to move away from the mindset that the "employee must have brought it upon himself" through some shortcoming or provocation. Similarly, the employee may be labeled as a troublemaker, or senior management may claim the troubles are due to personality differences. Ultimately the complaining employee is usually seen as expendable, ignored, and consequently moves on or out (Olsen, 2008).

Rather than first seeking mediation to resolve bullying, the organization must first act to protect the complainant. A standard non-victimization clause should be part of any complaint process, followed by an investigation to clarify allegations of workplace bullying. If the allegation is against a senior manager, an external resource is better. If the allegation is found to have substance, the perpetrator should be given directives to change or leave. This process should then be managed as with other kinds of hazards. Indeed, Olsen (2008) stressed that WB should be treated as a serious infraction that has the potential to seriously harm its victim(s). While an employee may seek counseling if available, many counselors have been known to direct the employee back to the organization for help without considering the potential harm such a recommendation could unleash in terms of retaliatory responses from the bully or employer (Ferris, 2004). Thus, the counseling professor would merit from a thorough understanding of workplace bullying.

Although EAP (Employee Advisory Program) professionals do work to help employees and employers maintain a respectful workplace (Badzmierowski, 2005), their roles are often ill defined. "Some counselors refuse to listen to victims of bullying, and insist that counseling sessions be entirely focused on problems the victim has that led to the bullying. Their straddling of the fence between employee and management support exacerbates the conflict between competing interests" (Namie & Namie, 2003, p. 2). Counselors may find it difficult to differentiate between true bullying and a situation where an employee has a disagreement with his/her boss. Moreover, Cooper et al. (2001) noted that EAP, which was originally established to help alcoholics, is first and foremost an arm of the organization. Thus, its representatives—although perhaps knowledgeable in broad issues of organizational conflict—are unlikely to "bite the hand that feeds them" with any force. Thus, the burden of proof rests with the victim, who may be returned to an abusive situation with little remedy. Cooper et al. (2001) further noted that in situations where mediation can negotiate a solution, the culprit should not be identified; instead, the mediator should analyze what has happened and then establish an arrangement where both can continue to work together or separately in a climate of greater mutual respect.

Despite measures that organizations can and should adopt to prevent and alleviate bullying, many organizations will refuse to embrace these measures. Researchers find that only 1 in 20 work groups is fully supportive of its members, which statistically puts 19 out of 20 work groups at risk for bullying (Cooper et al., 2001). Rather than conflict avoidance, helping managers and others in power develop their emotional intelligence and deal with differences in more appropriate ways may alleviate bullying. But the burden lies with the victim as well, who should feel empowered to stand his/her ground and address conflict with the full support of coworkers and upper management.

Methodology

Workplace bullying—the repeated mistreatment of a single person or a group using verbal/nonverbal attacks, humiliation, and intimidation—is a serious and pervasive problem in many workplaces, but seems to be most prevalent in institutions such as prisons, hospitals, and the military due to their heavily top-down organizational hierarchy. In these settings, behaviors are often inculcated and passed down from one supervisor to the next; thus, workers come to accept these as normal day-to-day responses to conflict (Hoel & Salin, 2003). As a rule, the organizational culture defines the role of leadership (Schein, 1985). If a leader allows bullying to become embodied in the culture and does not eradicate it, he will be tacitly reinforcing bullying. "The bottom line for leaders is that if they do not become conscious of the cultures in which they are embodied, those cultures will manage them" (Schein, 1985, p. 375).

According to Lutzen-Sandwick (2005), more research is needed that goes beyond the focus of individuals and dyads. Researchers need to explore bullying as an organization-wide phenomenon that is supported or not by institutional norms, organizational dynamics and pressures that impinge upon organizational actors. Archer (1994) asserted that we need to make sense of bullying and its myriad outcomes in order to stop it. The problem, however, is the lack of qualitative studies that explore individual perceptions and experiences (Moustakas, 1994; Newman, 2003).

Workplace bullying puts the victim, bystanders, and organizational productivity at risk. In the case of the victim, he or she may suffer from a wide range of physical, emotional and career-derailing consequences if it is not addressed. Additionally, coworkers who are privy to WB are also subjected to fear, stress, and possible emotional exhaustion. They may also experience feelings of helplessness, since they usually can provide little support due to institutional pressure or fear of retribution (Furnham, 2004). Organizations also suffer negative consequences as a result of workplace bullying. Direct costs include staff turnover, increases in absenteeism, higher worker errors, and litigation costs. Indirect costs are reflected in productivity losses, bad publicity, higher compensation premiums, and rehabilitation expenses.

This qualitative, phenomenological research study utilized first-hand narratives to reveal the impacts of workplace bullying among a small cohort of mostly retired military personnel. Their responses also elucidated how certain organizational factors (e.g., its culture) contribute to workplace bullying. More detailed research in this area will benefit workers at all level of the organization by clarifying the types of organizational structures and cultures that enable the problem to occur and propagate—as well as ways to eradicate bullying for the benefit of victim, coworkers, and the greater organization. Without such knowledge, bullies are likely to continue to terrorize workplaces and suffer few, if any, consequences.

CHAPTER 3.

METHODOLOGY

Chapter Three is divided into six sections. The first section details the methodological design of this investigation. The second section describes the procedures for selecting participants, the criteria for selection of participants, and their demographic information. Data collection techniques, which entailed the use of in-depth, semi-structured interviews, are explained in the third section. The fourth section discusses how the data was analyzed. The fifth section addresses the concepts of validity and reliability, and the final section addresses how the researcher managed ethical considerations, including how the anonymity of the participants was maintained, and the risks for taking part in this study were minimized (Marshall & Rossman, 1989).

Although Cowie et al. (2002) stressed the seriousness of the problem of bullying in society and the importance of developing proper techniques to capture its nature and measure its incidence, neither are straightforward in terms of approach. Cowie et al. (2002) indicated that not only is bullying difficult to define and evaluate accurately due to inappropriate measurement techniques, but not all bullying is "downward." Bullying may also be "upward" (when a subordinate bullies a boss) and "horizontal" (when bullying occurs between peers or colleagues (Lewis & Sheeham, 2003). This study employed a phenomenological qualitative research design to explore the complexity of workplace bullying.

Qualitative Research Methods

Dilts-Harryman (2007) stressed that more subjective qualitative studies of workplace bullying are needed to gather data on the essential meaning or reality of bullying from the perspective of victims. Similarly, Trochim et al. (2008) asserted that qualitative research is appropriate for investigating complex and sensitive issues. Moreover, due to its fluid nature (e.g., via the use of semi-structured interview questions) it can also cover a broader scope, thereby ensuring that some useful data is always generated (Experiment Resources (2008)."The design must remain flexible, because it will probably change throughout the research process" (Marshall & Rossman, 1989, p. 26). This flexibility allows for refining the process and the creation of knowledge.

Qualitative research design is typically used to study the experiential behaviors or experiences of humans. Thus, qualitative research studies are based on (or related to) experiences, attitudes, beliefs, or opinions instead of on statistically-verifiable evidence or phenomena (Trochim et al., 2008). Thomas (1949) noted that this research method is essential in understanding how people interpret certain situations; as he stated: "If men define situations as real, they are real in their consequences" (p. 301).

As an experience or situation, however, it can be difficult to differentiate workplace-bullying practices from "normal" workplace interactions (Daniel, 2009). According to Rayner and Melvor (2008) when constructs such as workplace bullying are unclear, "Research that uses in-depth, qualitative methodology can explore such constructs, rather than attempting to confirm the researcher's (potentially mistaken) view of the world" (p. 9). Qualitative research methods, therefore, often require supplementary research methods such as grounded theory research methods or the critical incident technique method to increase validity.

Grounded theory methods supplement qualitative research methods by providing "…systematic yet flexible guidelines for collecting and analyzing qualitative data to construct theories grounded in the data themselves"

(Charmaz, 2006, p. 2). This method usually entails developing categories from the responses of research participants. The type of qualitative method used for this research was *The Critical Incident Technique (CIT)*. According to Chell (2003), this method has been developed to serve as an investigative tool in organizational analysis from within an interpretative or phenomenological paradigm.

Design

Flanagan (1954) defined the Critical Incident Technique as set of procedures for collecting direct observations of human behavior in such a way as to facilitate their potential usefulness in solving practical problems and developing broad psychological principles. In this context, an "incident" is defined as any specific human activity that is sufficiently complete in and of itself to be scrutinized as a distinct phenomenon. Workplace bullying is such an activity—and a growing one at that. In exploring the effects of workplace bullying among a selected cohort of military personnel, the participants were asked to describe how bullying negatively impacted their physical health, psychological health, interpersonal relationships, self-confidence, self-esteem, job satisfaction, and careers. CIT was used to conduct in-depth interviews with them in order to acquire data from their personal perspectives. Such knowledge was expected to provide a more in-depth understanding of how to identify and manage the challenges arising from workplace bullying. Moreover, the CIT method was used to develop a classification system of critical incidents based on the degree of objectivity of observations. Objectivity is corroborated when two or more independent observers come to the same conclusions; Specifically, "The accuracy and therefore the objectivity of the judgments depend on the precision with which the characteristic has been defined and the competence of the observer in interpreting this definition with relation to the incident observed" (Flanagan, 1954, p. 9).

According to Flanagan (1954) there are five steps involved with CIT:

1. Determining the general aim of the study or introducing the study's objective with a brief statement;
2. Planning and specifying how factual incidents regarding the general aim of the study will be collected;
3. Collecting the data via oral interviews or written surveys;
4. Analyzing the data in such a way that it supports the goals of the study;
5. Interpreting and reporting the data once it has been categorized or classified.

Byrne (2001) listed three assumptions commonly associated with CIT: "First, the term critical incident refers to a clearly-demarcated scene. Second, if a detailed account of what actually happened cannot be obtained, that incident is not valid. Third, the critical incident itself is the basic unit of analysis" (p. 209). Although some protest that CIT is too rigid and narrowly prescribed to fully identify the complexities of human behavior, Flanagan (1954) asserted that CIT should be viewed as a flexible set of principles that can be modified and adapted to meet the specified situation. The critical incident technique is, therefore, highly appropriate for exploring topics that require participants to share their personal experiences, thought processes, and feelings regarding an incident (Chell, 2003). Chell (2003) added that "The objective is to gain an understanding of the incident from the perspective of the individual, taking into account cognitive, affective and behavioral elements" (p. 48). Assumptions using this approach include the fact that phenomena are best understood by viewing them in their context and a single unified reality exists outside our perception (Trochim et al., 2008).

According to Welman and Kruger (1999), a phenomenological approach is concerned with understanding the social and experiential phenomena from the perspective of those involved. Data captured from one or more interviews can help researchers understand people's experiences from their point of view (Kvale, 1996). At the root of phenomenology, "the intent is to understand the phenomena in their own terms—to provide a description of human experience as it is experienced by the person herself" (Bentz & Shapiro, 1998, p. 96), as well as to enable the essence of a phenomenon to emerge (Cameron, Schaffer & Park, 2001). According to Edmund Hussel, the father of phenomenology, this approach is designed to "backup things themselves"(as cited in Kruger and Stones, 1981, p. 28).

Limitations of phenomenological research mostly concern its generalizability, since the data acquired may ultimately only be applicable to a small group of participants (Ayoko, Callan, & Hartel, 2003; Mikkelson & Einarsen, 2002). Another limitation is that some interviewees may be reluctant to be completely candid due to the guilt and shame associated with victimization; as a result, they may not give accurate responses in order to present themselves in a more desirable way (Matthiesen & Einarsen, 2004). Similarly, Hoel and Rayner (1997) noted that a participant's self-report may be biased and not accurately reflect their true experiences.

Sampling Strategies

Selection of samples using the CIT approach involves first specifying how factual incidents that support the general goals of the study will be collected (Byrne, 2001). Accordingly, "Well-developed sampling decisions are crucial for any study's soundness" (Marshall & Rossman, 1989, p. 58). Additionally, purposive sampling is used when the researcher has a specific purpose for selecting a group of participants. The researcher must first determine that the respondents meet the criteria for being in the sample. In this instance, participant selection was based on whether or not they experienced or witnessed workplace bullying. However, this study required a "…relatively precise definition of each critical behavior category" (Flanagan, 1954, p.18). Respondents had to identify themselves as having experienced workplace bullying based on the definition provided by the Workplace Bullying Institute (2014). Specifically, WB is repeated, health-harming mistreatment of one or more persons (the targets) by one or more perpetrators that takes one of or more of the following forms: (a) verbal abuse, (b) offensive conduct/behaviors (including nonverbal) that are threatening, humiliating or intimidating; and (c) work interference/ sabotage that prevents work from getting done.

The data was collected using the Non-Probability Theoretical Sampling Method (i.e., using purposeful, non-random sampling). Specifically, the volunteer sample included military veterans, who either responded to posters placed at a veteran's retreat center inviting them to participate, or veterans who responded to invitations sent to members of a Veteran's of Foreign Wars organization. Those who were selected all acknowledged having been bullied. According to Hoepfl (1997), the decision as to when stop sampling is dependent on the research goals, the need to achieve depth through triangulation of data, and the possibility of increased breath after examining a variety of sampling sites. Ultimately, the sample size for this investigation consisted of 13 participants, all of whom were assigned pseudonyms and ensured of full confidentiality.

Data Collection

The primary forms of data collection in qualitative research consist of observations and conducting interviews (Marshall & Rossman, 1989). Accordingly, this investigation relied on the use of semi-structured, open-ended interviews as the primary strategy for data collection, which allowed for individual variations (Bogdon & Biklen, 1982). As described earlier, the Critical Incident Technique was employed, which required interviewees to identify incidents that they considered to be critically significant to their bullying experiences (Flanagan, 1954).

In terms of the study's protocol, letters of invitation were distributed to participants either by mail or electronic communication. The participant was continuously educated about the study from the point of initial contact to the completion of the study. Technical and medical terminology was avoided or explained in "lay" language, and materials were written at the eighth grade or lower reading level. Once the interview began, the discussion was guided and moderated rather than led. The interviews for this study were semi-structured to allow participants the opportunity to provide as much detailed information as needed to explore any concerns or provide additional information (Byrne, 2001). It should be noted that the interview protocols for this study were tested and refined to eliminate redundancies to ensure that each interview could be completed within 60 minutes. Specifically, the researcher field-tested the interview with two persons prior to conducting the full study.

Thirteen in-depth interviews were conducted by telephone. Although I had hoped to audio-record all thirteen, only three agreed to do so. For the remaining ten participants, I took copious notes, which resulted in hand-written narratives. Specifically, participants were asked if they have been negatively affected by their bullying experiences—and if so, how it may have affected their physical health, psychological health, self-esteem, job satisfaction/career, interpersonal relationships, and organizational productivity. They were also asked if they felt the culture of their workplace contributed to their experience of being a victim or witness of workplace bullying. The following six questions served as the basis for the interview, with two additional questions used to expand my understanding of the impact of workplace bullying.

RQ1. How has workplace bullying affected the employee's physical health?

RQ2. How has workplace bullying affected the employee's psychological health?

RQ3. How has workplace bullying affected the employee' self-esteem?

RQ4. How has workplace bullying affected the employee's interpersonal relationships?

RQ5. How has workplace bullying affected the employee's job satisfaction and career?

RQ6. How has workplace bullying affected the employee's organizational productivity?

These questions served as a "guide," enabling the researcher to introduce additional probes focusing on areas of particular importance as needed Also important to note is that although most of the participants were recruited from organizations that served former military personnel, most of the answers they provided pertained to their work-life in civilian organizations.

Qualitative researchers are held to few restrictions when it comes to when to stop the data collection process. Guba (1978) stated that the decision to terminate data collection should be based on exhaustion of resources, the emergence of patterns, or a trend toward overextension—i.e., extending beyond the boundaries of the research goals. Overall, the resulting data included the participants' position, his or her work environment, instances of specific mistreatment, the perceived impact of bullying on the organization, and the employer's response to the bullying situation. Caution was taken in presenting information about demographics in areas of ethnicity and class because inaccurate assumptions may be concluded from the data.

Data Analysis

Regardless of the strength of data collected in a qualitative investigation, the absence of a well-designed method of analysis will inevitably reduce its validity. "Qualitative data analysis provides an opportunity for the researcher to gain information and gather insights that may be overlooked with traditional data analytic techniques" (Lawrence & Tar, 2013, p. 29). Common approaches in analyzing qualitative data include hermeneutics, content analysis and semiotics (Myers, 1997).

Simply defined, hermeneutics is concerned with finding the meaning of text through interpretation which, in the sense relevant to hermeneutics, is an attempt to make clear, to make sense of an object of study. This object must, therefore, be a text, or a text-analogue, which in some way is confused, incomplete, cloudy, seemingly contradictory—in one way or another, unclear. The interpretation aims to bring to light an underlying coherence or sense. (Taylor, 1976, p. 153).

Content analysis is an approach use to interpret meaning from the content of the text data and develop objective coding schemes from the data (Hsieh & Shannon, 2005). "Semiotics is the science of signs, a sign being anything that can be used to stand for something else (Berger, 2014, p. 22). The key challenge is then placing raw data into logical, meaningful categories to examine them in a holistic fashion, and then to communicate the findings to others (Hoepfl, 1997).

There are five phases in the analytic process: (1) organizing the data; (2) generating categories, themes and patterns; (3) testing emerging hypothesis against the data; (4) searching for alternate explanations from the data; and (5) writing the report (Marshall & Rossman, 1989). According to Flanagan (1954), if a researcher has designed an investigation well, the data collection phase will be greatly simplified. Flanagan further stated, "A necessary condition for this phase is that the behaviors or results observed be evaluated, classified, and recorded while the facts are still fresh in the mind of the observer" (p. 13).

As noted above, of the 13 interviews I conducted (all via telephone), only 3 participants agreed to have their interviews audio-recorded. Thus, for the remaining 10 I had to take extensive notes during the interview. The 3 recorded interviews were transcribed verbatim and reviewed for accuracy, and each line of the transcript was numbered to aid in coding and analysis (Brown, 1996). The first step in organizing the data for this study was to listen and re-listen to available recorded data to review for accuracy and to become more familiar with the responses. I also read and reread all written data (transcriptions and interview notes). Analysis began with "open coding" or by identifying themes emerging from the raw data (Strauss & Corbin, 1998).

The second phase, generating categories, themes, and patterns "… demands a heightened awareness of the data, a focused attention to those data, and an openness to the subtle, tacit, undercurrents of social life. Identifying salient themes, recurring ideas or language, and patterns of belief that link people and settings together…" (Marshall & Rossman, 1989, p. 115). As categories emerge, the researcher then identifies the salient categories of meaning conveyed by the participants (Patton, 1980). Patton (1980) asserted that the researcher must uncover… "what is really significant and meaningful in the data" (p. 113).

By testing emergent hypotheses during the third phase, important categories and patterns eventually can be identified from the data (Marshall and Rossman, 1989), which "entails a search through the data, challenging the hypothesis, searching for negative instances of the pattern, and incorporating these into larger constructs, if necessary" (p. 118). According to Goffman (1959), the researcher must approach qualitative data with some skepticism, even though rigorous procedures may have been used to gain truthful information. Due to the fact that participants may have expressed a particular presentation of themselves during the interview (i.e., told the interviewer what they thought he/she wanted to hear or was selective in what they shared), the researcher must be thorough in searching for alternative interpretations of the data—which represents the fourth phase of the analytical process. The researcher collected and analyzed the data. Data was reviewed to determine if it was useful in illuminating the research question or if the information was irrelevant and should be reexamined or discarded. The data was categorized and recurring themes that emerged from the data were identified. The fifth and final phase of the process is reflected in this document—writing up the report.

Ethical Considerations

"An essential element of all good research is that it be done in an ethical manner, with careful planning and procedures to protect the individuals who participate" (Devlin, 2001, para. 3). Researchers are responsible for maximizing the benefits of the data that participants are willing to share, while at the same time minimizing any harm to them. Researchers need to understand that participants may be adjusting their priorities and routines to help the researcher (Marshall & Rossman, 1989), thereby heightening the need to ensure that any inconvenience is minimized. Most important, the emotional health of participants must be considered throughout the investigation. "Most research that pinpoints the costs of bullying glosses over the emotional pain of abuse" (Tracey, 2004, p. 153). With this in mind, the length of the interview was limited to one hour to avoid exposing them possible emotional exhaustion. Additionally, the researcher used caution in utilizing words and phrases that may have triggered emotional responses. For example, in some cases use of the word "bullying" was avoided because it elicited feelings of inferiority or inadequacy. "Individuals often blame themselves for being targeted and have trouble creating coherent story lives that persuasively and succinctly convey their situation"(Tracey, 2004, p. 154).

As a caseworker for a social services organization, the researcher for this study has had training in interviewing respondents about sensitive and emotionally-charged issues while at the same time addressing three important ethical issues: informed consent, the right to privacy and confidentiality, and protection of participants from harm (Punch, 1986; Jacobs, 1987; Fontaren & Frey, 1994). Informed consent is a key concern and requires more than just obtaining a participant's signature. Every participant needs a clear understanding of what it means to participate in the investigation (Partners Human Research, 2010)—principally, that participants will be accurately informed about the research so that they may make clear and conscious choices about whether or not they wish to participate (Hammersley & Athinson, 1995; Davis, 1989). The Informed Consent Form (Appendix A) is vital to the research process. It contains information describing the extent to which the researcher will play a role as a participant in the research; it must also clearly detail how the data will be collected from participants, and how it will be maintained to ensure confidentiality (and for how long it will be maintained). Ethical concerns and informed consent must be discussed with participants prior to scheduling interviews. The rights to privacy and confidentiality require the protection of one's identity and research setting both during and after the study (Punch, 1994; Adler & Adler, 1994).

The third broad code, protection from harm, pertains to ensuring that no participant suffers as a result of taking part in the research (Kelman, 1982; Hammersley & Atkinson, 1995; Vanderstaay, 2005). "Protecting the human research participant is more important than the pursuit of new knowledge. It takes precedence over the personal or professional gain of the researcher" (Devlin, 2001, para 15). Protection from harm includes physical and psychological harm, as well as any harm that results from publishing of the findings—such as the undermining of personal and organizational reputations (Hammersley & Atkinson, 1995; Punch, 1994). This study was designed to minimize any harm to participants and findings will be presented accurately, while at the same time protect the identity and confidentiality of participants (Devlin, 2001).

Validity and Reliability

Critics of qualitative research are prone to cite validity issues as a main concern (Winter, 2000). In anticipation of this concern, "member checking," an interactive method for establishing validity was conducted—for example, by enabling participants to review transcripts or notes and have them provide feedback about the study. In some cases, certain interviewees worked with the researcher in the planning, conducting, and analyzing of results. And as noted earlier, reliability was enhancing by listening to the available audio-recordings multiple times. In reviewing the resulting response categories according to the coded data assigned to each category, the researcher confirmed validity with at least 75% accuracy.

Reliability of content analysis refers to the stability and consistency of the research findings—i.e., the frequency with which a given instrument is likely to produce the same results regardless of the participant cohort. The researcher was able to determine the level of reliability because of test-retest procedures that reinforces the dependability of research findings.

Summary

Chapter 3 outlined the method, plan, and purpose of this research study. To reiterate, this study was designed to determine the outcomes of workplace bullying within a cohort of 13 former military personnel using a phenomenological qualitative research approach. This method was deemed to be appropriate for a study of this type that canvasses the experiences of a small number of individuals who provided highly subjective responses to complicated and sensitive questions. This study utilized telephone interviews as the source of data, which was then examined in light of available literature findings addressing the effects of workplace bullying. The results of this study, which are detailed in Chapter Four, indicate that workplace bullying is a persistent problem that organizations tend to address minimally, if at all. This realization could stimulate discussions about the pernicious quality of WB, not to mention how organizations can address this issue—or, better yet, create an environment that precludes the possibility of it ever occurring.

CHAPTER 4.

RESULTS

Background

The purpose of this qualitative phenomenological investigation was to explore the lived experiences of people who had either been the targets of workplace bullies or who had witnessed first-hand the effects of workplace bullying. This study was designed to determine how WB impacted a small cohort of participants in six areas: physical health, psychological health, self-esteem, interpersonal relationships, career impacts/aspirations, and organizational productivity. An eight-question instrument (Appendix C) was used to solicit data. During telephone interviews—only three of which were transcribed verbatim—participants described their individual experiences with WB and made inferences as to how it impacted the areas listed above.

The positivist approach originated with social science theory and was used to analyze the data according to a simplified version of the Stevick-Colaizzi-Keen method, as referenced in Creswell (2006). The researcher conducted comprehensive telephone interviews using semi-structured questions. As noted earlier, three were audio-recorded and transcribed verbatim. For the remaining ten, I took copious notes to gain a more thorough understanding of the participants' feelings, thoughts, attitudes and concerns as they related to the research questions (Pina, 2005). During the in-depth telephone interviews, participants described their WB experiences, revealing how it may have impacted their health, self-esteem, view of their organization, and any other outcomes that would help to reveal how it impacted their lives.

Participant Profiles

This study canvassed the experiences of 13 participants, all military veterans, ranging in age from 28 to 73 years (average age 58) with respect to WB. Two participants were retired from the military; one was still active duty in the U.S. Navy. The remaining 10 had served their tours and moved into civilian life and work. The participants varied with respect to educational attainment: one had earned a doctorate; one was pursuing a doctorate, one had an M.S.; five held bachelor's degrees; and the others were all high school graduates. As noted, most of the interviewees were retired: two from the military, two from owning their own businesses, one from state social services, another had been a high school principal, one was a construction worker and the final retiree was a shipyard employee. The participants who still worked (three hospital service workers, a management consultant, and a social service worker) had at some point all served in the Navy. Based on information from the Demographic Questionnaire (Appendix B), the characteristics of this study's cohort are provided in Table 5.

Table 4:

Demographics of Participants

NAME	Gender	Age 28-55	Age 56-73	Educational Level	Employment
Debra	Female	yes		Master's Degree	Social Services
Leonard	Male	yes		Bachelor's Degree	Medical Technology
Steve	Male	yes		Doctorate Degree	Business Management
James	Male		yes	Some College	Military retiree
Rick	Male		yes	High School graduate	Laundry worker
999	Male	yes		Some College	Medical Technology
Emily	Female		yes	Some College	Bus Driver
Joseph	Male		yes	Some College	Military retiree
Mike	Male		yes	Master's Degree	HS School Principal
Charles	Male	yes		Bachelor's Degree	Document Analysis

Kenneth	Male	yes	Some College	Business Entrepreneur (retired)
Leon	Male	yes	High School Graduate	Construction Worker (retired)
Phillip	Male	yes	High School graduate	Business Entrepreneur

To protect their confidentiality, participants were assigned pseudonyms and their narratives are presented in block quote format. Their pseudonyms and years of experience (xx) in civilian organizations are as follows: *Steve (15); Leonard (20); Kenneth (40); Phillip (30); Rick (25); Leon (42); Debra (20); Emily (25); James (22); Mike (30); Joseph (40); Charles (4); and Wayne (10)*.

Questions, Responses and Analysis

The participants were asked to respond to the following six open-ended questions that guided the development of this study:

RQ1. How has workplace bullying affected the employee's physical health?

RQ2. How was workplace bullying affected the employee's psychological health?

RQ3. How has workplace bullying affected the employee' self-esteem?

RQ4. How has workplace bullying affected the employee's job satisfaction or career?

RQ5. How has workplace bullying affected the employee's productivity in the workplace?

RQ6. How has workplace bullying affected the employee's interpersonal relationships?

Note that the questions were modified down during the interview process to target specific aspects of WB outcomes—e.g., physical versus psychological outcomes, as well as several other modifications. Moreover, additional probes were added as needed to clarify answers and eliminate ambiguities. Their responses were recorded independently under strict confidentiality by the researcher. In limited cases responses were also audiotaped.

Q1. How has workplace bullying affected your physical health?

The majority of the respondents identified stress resulting from bullying as leading to actual or potential health problems they may have experienced.

Debra was a government social services employee. She had worked in her field for over 20 years. She was eager to relate a bullying experience she had while working on a temporary job project.

I can only recall one time. It was a project I was working on. I was only there about 10 months and I left because I had so many knots in my back and neck because of my supervisor being a micro manager and just moody to everybody. A lot of people had trouble with him. I had knots in my back and neck that I never had before. I had to go for massage therapy for a couple of months. I decided my health was more important than my job, so I left. I had to go someplace else.

Steve held a doctorate degree and worked as a management consultant. He also commented on the stress associated with WB.

Workplace bullying creates a lot of stress. There is stress in observing a stressful environment. It creates anxiety and all that stuff.

James is was a military retiree. He had worked in a government hospital for over 20 years.

The stress caused high blood pressure and aggravated the rotator cuff in my shoulder. I had to have surgery on my shoulder. The bullying aggravated my tendinitis and my arthritis. I think it affected my blood pressure. When I was bullied, I felt pain in my arms and legs at different times at work. When I started to see the doctor, he [the doctor] told me my problems were mainly due to stress. Once I was told I would be in charge of the kitchen, and worked temporarily in that position; but when the actual hiring took place, they gave the position to someone else. This was really stressful because I am a very hard worker. Some of the hospital staff would come into the kitchen and would demand food and things and were very rude. They came in at different hours so it was difficult to be prepared to provide what they were wanting.

Emily had worked for almost 20 years at a veteran's hospital. She wanted to learn more about bullying and help to eliminate the problem.

It caused stress. I started feeling kind of depressed, worried and weary. I had nervousness and it caused stomach problems and diarrhea.

Mike was a retired high school principal. He said most of his experiences were in positions prior to working in the field of education, he said:

It caused me to have stomach problems and headaches.

Rick is a veteran from the Vietnam War era and worked for a Veteran's hospital.

I am bullied on my job. Sometimes I have problems going to sleep and have to take sleeping pills.

Charles worked as a contractor in Iraq where he experienced bullying.

Bullying creates a lot to of stress It didn't affect me physically in anyway.

Analysis of Responses to Question 1: The majority of participants linked workplace bullying to stress when referring to physical ailments. According to Field (1996), these physical health symptoms are usually not linked, at least initially, to workplace bullying. Physical symptoms resulting from stress include tearfulness, headaches, colds, coughs, susceptibility to illnesses, susceptibility to infections, flu-like symptoms, and aches and pain. Researchers have also linked stress from workplace bullying as leading to higher body weight and heart disease—not to mention a veritable laundry list of other physical conditions (Cooper & Marshall, 1976; Kivimak et al., 2003; Simon, 2010).

According to Lazurus and Folkman (1984), the nature and severity of reactions following exposure to a stressor are functions of a dynamic interplay between the specific characteristics of events, and the individual's appraisal and coping processes. An individual's personality and coping mechanisms help to moderate or determine the health and well-being of those exposed to stressors. A term used to describe healthy coping mechanisms is *Psychological Hardiness*. Stressors can cause *cognitive dissonance* when a discrepancy between what one expects to happen and what actually happens—or between how one perceives himself and how one is perceived by another—should occur (Ursin &Eriksen, 2004). When Individuals view these discrepancies as manageable, they are less likely to develop health risks as a result of stress. On the other hand, if stressors are viewed as unmanageable, the level of physical activation increases.

Research studies have found that an inability to manage stressful situations (e.g., WB) causes high stress levels and pathological problems such as decreased sleep, increased cortisol levels, elevated heart rate and mortality. Secondary outcomes include increased absenteeisms from work and reduced performance (Mikkelsen et al., 2002; Nieslen et al., 2008). Bies and Tripp (2005) posited the Theories of Revenge and Reactions in response to personal injustices. When targets perceive an absence of protection from harm in the workplace, their coping mechanisms are likely to be negatively impacted. Thus, the lack of support from senior management and/or coworkers put them at risk for anger and disillusionment—not only with the bully, but with organization itself. Victims develop job dissatisfaction and may decide to quit (Willness, Steel, & Lee, 2007). To reiterate, although the bully is the primary source of stress in the workplace, the situation is exacerbated when coworkers and HR/ senior management do nothing to stop it. Low-level stress, if left unabated, can escalate, which prevents rational, controlled action with the possibility of resulting in overwhelmingly negative consequences (WBI, 2014).

Q2. How has workplace bullying affected your psychological health?

The most common theme arising in responses to Question 2 identified stress as the greatest threat to psychological health. James even said he suffered a minor degree of PTSD due to workplace bullying.

James: *I would think about it –why was this happening? I felt uncomfortable with my supervisor looking over my shoulder and when he saw I could do my work, he walked away with a smudge on his face. Sometimes I think I would flare up at home because of the pressure. It was causing me to drink alcohol. I thought at the time it was helping the situation. I would drink after a bad day, but I discovered it wasn't helping the situation.*

Emily: *It causes stress. When I first started, it made me feel depressed, but now I am used to it. I still get upset because sometimes my supervisor says Emily you can't do that, while others do the same thing and she said nothing. I am a little irritated when I leave this job. Sometimes I hate to go into her office or be around her because I feel she is going to aggravate me. I never know from one day to the next how she will be.*

Mike: *Under supervision of director of school district, the supervisor bullied the whole school district. I was going to leave. I had requested a conference with my supervisor.*

Debra: *Not so much psychological. I will just say that when you are in a position where you are bullied, you may second-guess yourself. You have this person who is constantly scrutinizing you may know you are doing a good job, but have a lot of negative things said about you. You have this person who scrutinizes everything you do. It may be psychological because you feel that you are not performing at the level you should be or that you are not good enough for that task.*

Steve: *You begin to question yourself. You are in an intense conflict situation and you must work through the process. A fight- or- flight reaction starts up. You ask yourself, what part of this is my fault? What part of this is my responsibility?*

Wayne: Wayne was active-duty military at the time this study was conducted. He was supervised by a female colonel who apparently used bullying, which created tension:

It creates tension, makes you lose respect. My supervisor bullies. She has caused me to disrespect her and still she is supervisor. She is retired from the Navy so I hate to hear from co-workers how she treats me. It is a poor reflection of naval laws.

Charles: *You just get stressed. I didn't let it bother me. I did not get depressed or anything but I used to think about it after work and sometimes it would create minor anxiety.*

Rick: *Psychologically, not yet. God keeps me in the right frame of mind. I talked to my psychologist and he told me not to take it personally and not to shift blame as it is my responsibility. God keeps me in right frame of mind.*

Analysis of responses to Question 2. These responses relate to Field's (1996) contention that obsessiveness with the situation, hypersensitivity to criticism or implied criticism or remarks increases self-depreciation and self-effacements. These are symptomatic of bullied experiences. To be a victim of intentional and systematic psychological harm, be it real or perceived, seems to produce severe health problems in the target when the bullying occurs on a regular basis (Einarsen & Rakness, 1997; Vartia, 2001).

Steve referenced the fight-or-flight response that occurs in the first of three stages of stress. The body reacts to threats of an impending sense of danger. This alarm triggers the sympathetic nervous system that releases adrenalin to deal with the stress (Namie & Namie, 2000). The second stage is characterized by resistance to stress, which occurs so the body can continue to function normally. However, if the bullying is continuous, the body's defense system can become depleted, causing a full system breakdown (Namie & Namie, 2000).

Randall (1997) identified some core psychological symptoms associated with stress:

- Feelings and actions associated with beliefs of experiencing stressful event
- Tense psychological stress occurring when exposed to traumatic events
- Nightmares, difficulty sleeping, poor concentration, irritability and other psychological deficits when exposed to stimuli reminiscent of the trauma
- Aggressive behavior, moodiness and feelings of guilt

Victims reported experiencing sleep problems, low self-esteem, anxiety, concentration difficulties, chronic fatigue, anger, depression and somatic problems (e.g. Brodsky, 1976; Einarsen & Raknes, 1997; Einarsen et al., 1994). According to Zapf (1996), exposure to personalized attacks is strongly correlated with mental health problems. However, caution must be taken with self-reported information of this nature, since the actual source of the stress could be external to the workplace; alternatively, multiple sources of stress may be exacerbating a bullying situation that might otherwise be manageable.

James admitted to having experienced Post Traumatic Stress Disorder (PTSD) due to the bullying he had experienced. A PTSD diagnosis refers to a build-up of stress symptoms typically exhibited by victims of exceptionally traumatic events (APA, 2000). The victim relives the incidents and experiences intense psychological discomfort. The victim may have a physical reaction when reminded or the event or avoid any stimuli related to the event. Mitchell (2010) confirmed that bullying causes PTSD because the trauma associated with it is not an isolated, short-term event. Indeed, bullying can manifest itself as a long-term or chronic event that spans a period of months or even years.

Trauma of this nature may even change one's concept of who they are and their ability to cope with stressful situations (Mitchell, 2010).

People exposed to long-term traumas can be thought of as being held in physical and/or emotional captivity. They are unable to free themselves from the influence of their abuser. Examples include people held in prisoner-of-war camps, those who experience long-term domestic violence, and those experiencing repeated physical abuse and childhood sexual abuse. Researchers believe that workplace bullying should included in this list and be more precisely identified as Complex PTSD (C-PTSD), which is characterized by trauma that is repeated or long term (Mitchell, 2010).

Studies also indicate that victims of bullying tend to make less use of problem-solving strategies to improve their situations in comparison non-victims (Hogh & Dofradottir, 2001), which is no doubt connected to negative psychological implications of stress. Conversely, Zapf & Gross (2001) discovered that victims could succeed in improving their situation when they recognized and properly challenged escalatory bullying behavior.

Medical practitioners often misdiagnose illnesses when victims seek treatment (Einarsen, 2000; Leymann & Gutavsou, 1996). It is extremely important that they become knowledgeable of the symptoms. For example, practitioners need to recognize that victimization-related PTSD is largely due to the shattering of basic assumptions victims hold about themselves and the world (Janoff-Bulmann, 1992). James, for example, sought advice from a counselor for symptoms of PTSD. According to James, the counselor failed to acknowledge any problems that could have stemmed from WB—but may not have been fully trained to recognize them. The counselor was only concerned about stress that would have resulted from military combat.

Q3. How has workplace bullying affected your self-esteem?

Most of the participants said in the face of tremendous workplace criticism, their self-esteem may have been negatively impacted, which causes them to second-guess themselves and lose faith in their decisions.

Debra*: It makes you second-guess myself due to the tremendous criticism. I received constant criticism. I said my health is more important than my job, so I left to lessen the impact and to let him know I mean business. You are not going to mistreat me. Nobody else knows you are going through this when you meet with him one on one. Person is constantly badgering you saying you need to take a writing class, or I didn't like your emails.*

Steve*: You begin to second-guess yourself. Is this real? Why is this happening?*

Wayne*: It made me feel like I was losing my dignity by staying on the job. Charles: It makes you feel you are not very good if your supervisor keeps intimidating you. It probably affected my relationships with co-workers because we all felt we were mistreated. Some of my co-workers even had resentment for the system. Some have been shown disrespect because they had been bullied verbally or had things said to them by management that showed disrespect. Others were given extra work to do. The one good thing is they couldn't just fire you without approval from upper management.*

James*: It made you think you are doing poorly. My boss would stand over me and watch as if I didn't know what I was doing. He was trying to belittle me. He would not make a comment. He would just walk away when he found it was satisfactory. My boss didn't have the technical knowledge I had learned in school. He would say, I have never seen it done that. It made me feel very uncomfortable. I felt he was antagonizing me. I was experienced in my job and knew what I was doing. Others even told him that.*

Emily: *A co-worker yelled at me like I was a child and made me feel inferior. He didn't have to talk to me like I was an idiot. I was almost in tears. My boss sometimes comes along and tries to tear down my accomplishments when I am doing the best I can. She makes you feel intimidated. She will go along with anything her boss says and acts like she is afraid of her. She even said one time, that her boss would not allow us to take leave. I still get upset because sometimes my supervisor says Emily you can't do that, while others do the same thing and she said nothing. I am a little irritated when I leave this job. Sometimes I hate to go into her office or be around her because I feel she is going to aggravate me. I never know from one day to the next how she will be from one day to the next.*

Rick: *No, because I know who I am.*

Joseph (an air force retiree who has recently retired from self-employment): *In the air force a guy was bullying me. I went to the latrine put his head in the sink and poured water over him. He had taken me to the brink. He never bothered me again.*

Phillip (an Air Force retiree who is also a retired shipyard worker): *It did not bother me at all. It just taught me to treat people better regardless of color, size, shape, etc.,*

Analysis of Responses to Question 3: Self-esteem refers to one's positive evaluation about him/herself as a person (Harter, 1990; Rosenberg, 1965). Eight of the thirteen participants disclosed feelings of indignation and confusion when exposed to WB; they also reported second-guessing themselves. Some or all of the five participants whose self-esteem did not seem to be negatively impacted may have preferred not to recall such incidents. According to Randall (2001), victims of workplace bullying can be profoundly ashamed of being victimized and are confused by their apparent inability to fight back and protect themselves. Similarly, Swan (1983) proposed the Self-Verification Theory, which indicates that people have a strong need to engage in activities that align with and support positive self esteem—namely as highly competent, successful, and in control (Miner, 1992). In contrast, WB is likely to undermine all of these qualities.

According to Harvey (1996), workers subjected to bullying may become distracted from their sense of potency because of abuse, disrespect, and attacks on their competency. For example, Emily reported that she had been distracted from her job as a driver. Research also shows that bullying itself may affect decision-making because it erodes a person's faith in him/herself (Harvey, 1996). According to Zapf & Einarsen (2003), victims are less likely to fight back because the bully has subdued them. Targets often feel trapped and unable to respond for fear of losing their job. If they confront their bosses, they may be accused of near-mutiny, which further lowers their self-esteem (Harvey, 1996). In coping with this situation, targets can choose between two alternatives: work hard to avoid further criticism and badgering, or forego self-direction in favor of self- protection (Harvey, 1996).

Emily reported an attack upon her self-esteem by a co-worker. Although co-workers may not have the same powers as managers or supervisors, they often employ the same bullying tactics on their colleagues. In some cases, they feel this attack may earn rewards from perpetrators who have targeted their colleagues. They therefore hope to advance their careers by making co-workers appear weak and incompetent. Whatever their reasons, colleagues who bully are just as detrimental as bosses who bullying (Burgess, 2014).

Victims suffering from low self-esteem may be fearful of speaking up or exhibit obvious signs of tension, such as submissive body language, distracted doodling, eye-rolling, or exhibiting discomfort when the bully talks (Alsener, 2008). A victim's self esteem can be further undermined by the bully who takes credit for others' contributions, dominates meetings, uses sarcasm, interrupts, or used outright insults (Alsener, 2008). Moreover, when bullying has evolved to mobbing or when there are multiple attackers, they may disguise their attacks as humor. Mobbing also usually also manifests in such negative acts as social isolation, the silent treatment and rumors. Victims who develop psychological problems as a result of bullying and mobbing may experience nervous breakdowns, panic attacks, depression, loss of confidence and self-esteem, reduced ability to concentrate, vagueness, lack of motivation, suicidal thoughts, feelings of isolation and burnout (Yildiz, 2007). Additionally, prior research has found that targets may blame themselves for what has happened to them. They often have low levels of control over the situation and exhibit sadness (Siemer, Marcus, & Gross, 2007); in contrast, individuals have positive emotions such as joy and happiness when they feel in control, and their goals and objectives are being met.

Q4a. How has workplace bullying affected your job satisfaction or career?

Leon, Kenneth, Joseph and Emily said their bullying experience had no impact on their job satisfaction or career. However, participants Debra, Steve and James reported that it had *a tremendous impact* on job satisfaction.

Debra*: It affected me tremendously because I left. I just was there for a year And a half and didn't want to work there anymore. It lessened the impact on me to remain civil. I wanted him to know you are not going to mistreat me. I dreaded going to work. I told him, I am going to leave no matter what you say or do. He realized what he had done. I said no I still have to go.*

Steve*: Huge impact on job satisfaction. I need a healthy work environment and it affected my ability to engage in meaningful dialogues with people. I work in management consulting. Bullying makes it difficult to solve complex problems with people. I eventually changed jobs.*

Charles*: Others were having the same experiences so we worked cohesively and were able to share our experiences and no one confronted management about the bullying. Nothing would have been done about it probably. They could always replace you even though we were working in Iraq.*

Emily: *My boss came along once and said to me while I was on by lunch break that while I was waiting I could be parking cars. I said nothing because I was still on my break and she was just talking out of her mind. She does it a lot. She made this comment while she was walking. Some people just like to throw their weight around. It is about power and authority. She is always saying she loves her job. It is not me who lacks self- confidence, it is her.*

James: *Yes, when I realized my caliber and high standards and saw my boss's weren't as high as mine. I got kind of discouraged. He would not give the special instructions needed for some of the patients and then he would question me about not preparing the diets correctly. I finally began going directly to the nurses and doctors for the diet changes. I had to go to three different nurses when I got to work, rather than my supervisor. He didn't approach me about it after that. If I needed any clarification, the nurse would ask the dietician. My biggest problem was seeing children with special diets and the staff supervising kids did not always give them what they were supposed to have. The kids already had psychological issues, and they were causing medical issues too. That was stressful in itself.*

Analysis of responses to Question 4a. Emily's statement dovetails with research indicating that bullying and stress may actually re-wire the brain. Behavior used by the bully to humiliate, intimidate and frighten the target can cause a person to become unable to cope with daily tasks and meet requirements of the job (Einarsen, 2000). The experiences of Emily, James, Debra, and Steve are examples of long-lasting states of discomfort due to victimization that subsequently develops into job dissatisfaction, a lack of organizational commitment and intentions to leave the job (Einarsen & Raknes, 1997). Interestingly, Charles, in recalling cohesion among coworkers, may suggest that sharing experiences with others helps to build social support that can mitigate the effects of bullying. By sharing information, they may have been able to prevent escalation of conflict, thereby avoiding having to confront management. According to Zapf & Gross (2001), victims who succeed in improving their situation are (1) generally better at recognizing escalatory behaviors and thus avoiding them, and (2) are proactive in the face of bullying. Prior to that time, however, they may have also suffered silently out of fear of retribution and because it may have been difficult to fully explain what was happening and how it started (Richardson & McCord, 2001).

"Many targets seem to consider complaining about the bullying to be an act of *disloyalty to* their supervisor or the organization. This fact was recently borne out in the US Workplace Bullying of Survey 2007 wherein forty percent of the targets indicated that they never reported to their employer" (Daniel, 2009, p. 56). The interruptions that Steve and Emily described both affected their ability to do their job to the best of their abilities and cope successfully with daily tasks (Einarsen, 2000). Work interruptions are a common bully tactic. The purpose of unnecessary interruptions is to threaten, belittle and destabilize the victim. Attacks upon a person's professionalism can also be caused by "client bullies," which is when an employee is harassed by the people they set out to serve (e.g., teachers bullied by students; doctors/nurses bullied by patients; supervisors bullied by those who report to them). Clients who bully may do so for several reasons. One, they may feel threatened by the victim's credentials and respond aggressively. Clients may also feel this will elevate their standing among coworkers. However, research shows that such bullying is detrimental to all levels of the organization in terms of productivity and creativity (Cooper & Hoel, 2000).

Q4b. Did workplace bullying cause you to change your career? If so, how?

This additional question was added in the interview protocol to determine if bullying directed resulted in attrition. Among this group of interviewees, the bullying experience did not engender any direct career changes—which is not to say it had no effect. James indicated that it caused him to retire; Leonard indicated that he had been fired; and Steve changed companies.

Wayne: *Not yet, I am considering it. I approached her supervisor and he is making it appear that he is reprimanding her. So I hate to hear from all those co-workers how she treats me [treats all co-workers]. It is a poor reflection of navy laws.*

Steve: *No, not careers, changed companies.*

Debra: *I said I am not cut out for this. Then he realized what he had said, I can do this for you if you stay. He wanted to make plans for me to stay after he realized how nasty he had been. No one else could come in there and build those relationships overnight. I said no, nothing you can do or say will make me stay.*

Leonard (who works as a manager and technician in a military hospital): *I was fired unfairly from the post office and I was happy to leave. [He said jokingly]. It was probably the best thing that ever happened to me.*

James: *It forced me to retire or had a bearing on my retirement. The supervisor tried to give me a counseling about the mouse problem as if I were lying about the mice in the kitchen. I told him evidently I was telling the truth because seven other people saw them. I was only concerned about the health and welfare of the kids. They [management] tried to handle it internally and told management that I felt we needed professionals to come in and get rid of them. They really became angered about this because they were trying to save money. I refused to sign the counseling statement.*

Emily: *It is causing me to want to retire. I haven't retired yet but I am old enough to retire and am thinking about it.*

Rick: *You just keep your mouth shut and not let it affect you. The things they [the organization] should be concerned with, they are not concerned with.*

Analysis of responses to Question 4b. Most participants said the bullying did not cause them to change their jobs or careers. James reported that it caused him to retire early and Emily said she is contemplating retirement because of the bullying. A common thread from the responses is that targets are likely to be more tolerant of bullying when their financial options are limited. For example, Rick said: "You just have to keep your mouth shut and not let it affect you." Many employees choose to remain on the jobs because they feel they can cope with mild forms of bullying. Nonetheless research shows that even "benign" bullying can undermine one's self-confidence and trust in others. A study by Vartia (2001) indiciated that non-bullied co-workers who fear becoming the next victim report higher levels of stress and leave the organization more often than the targets.

Q5. Has workplace bullying affected your productivity or perspectives about the organization—and if so, how?

The majority of the participants said bullying changed the way they viewed management. They had not expected management to allow bullying. They also implied that management was usually unsupportive and refused to change. Leon, however, spoke positively about the construction industry. Interestingly, while studies support the contention that construction has one of the lower prevalence rates for workplace bullying, there are still problems for female participation in the workforce. Studies show women have been victims of discrimination, harassment and other barriers (Moir, Thompson, & Kelleher, 2011).

Steve*: Definitely, in the long term, bad organizations have this problem. Some companies have a gladiator-type of culture. In the long term this burns bridges. The environment is tainted with these problems.*

Debra*: Overall, yes it changed my opinion. I did not expect this. They are not inclusive it comes to ethnicity, religion, etc., I thought they really cared about their people. It is rather subtle, telling groups of people you are not good enough to be a part of the management team.*

You see people being promoted who don't look like you. Perhaps they are just this way to certain people.

Wayne*: It lowered the way I look at management.*

Charles*: Organizations are stiff. They were used to doing things a certain way and didn't want to change. I didn't expect to experience the bullying at work after I graduated from college.*

James*: They were doing what they wanted to do. A mouse fell on a nurse after I had often told them there was a mouse problem. I told them it was unsafe for the kids. They didn't believe me, as a matter of fact, I was counseled about it. They are not concerned with things they should be concerned with. A mouse fell on a nurse's head. They gave me a counseling over it about a month later. I did not sign the counseling statement. They didn't do anything. They did not want to mess with the union. They had to grounds to base it on. The organization was always concerned about trying to cut back on funds. It was always about money, not the kid's mental and physical problems. They had some staff in charge who were not medical professionals and should not have been handling some of the tasks.*

Emily*: People on job don't care about teamwork. I just wanted to work there. It made me mad and there is so much favoritism on the job.*

Rick*: Favoritism is very fluent. It is hard not to take it personally. I needed a break. It was reported to the chief. The assistant chief lied in his report and wrote it up as I had caused the problem when someone else had caused the problem.*

Leon (a retired construction worker who served in combat in Vietnam). *In the construction industry it was so rare, sometimes it happens now and then. It is more likely to happen if you are in a lower position. How you treated somebody—it always came around to that supervisor was no longer there.*

Analysis of responses to Question 5. Targets of workplace bullying generally develop a negative attitude about their organization (Namie, 2000). A common theme that emerged from this question is that participants perceived a low level of organizational support in dealing with WB. As a result, targets become increasingly humiliated in feeling more and more isolated and defenseless. Although upper management may not directly attack the target, leadership who turns a blind eye to bullying inevitably contributes to an environment of psychological threat. According to Hollander (1958, 1961), an organization will be more tolerant of deviant behavior as long as the bully contributes to meeting the organization's goals. Therefore, many organizations are willing to sacrifice an employee's morale and motivation for short- and long-term productivity goals. In the case of long-term "blindness," this then becomes an institutional norm. In the case of the victimized employee, powerlessness over a protected period of time becomes a of "learned helplessness."

Rick reported that his organization exhibited *fluent favoritism.* Dienesch and Liden (1986) and Graen and Uhl-Bien (1996) theorized that leader-member relationships exist on a continuum from low (role-taking) to high (routinization). Between those bookends is role-making. This theory is known as the LMX Theory, which was developed in the 1970s to describe the relationship stages between a leader and his/her subordinates. Subordinates who experience a high LMX relationship with a leader (the "in-group) are likely to be granted more advantages and regarded more favorably. Conversely, those who experience a poor relationship with management (the "out-group") have low quality exchanges, receive no advantages and are regarded unfavorably (e.g., Liden, Sparrow & Wayne, 1997). Moreover, the in-group receiving preferential treatment from supervisors is intrinsically motivated to maintain these productive relationships, which may cause them to be more tolerant of coworker bullying (Harris, Harvey, & Kacmar, 2011). The negative effects of WB can reach beyond the immediate target. Bullies can poison the entire workplace environment by creating low morale, fear, anger—all of which can lead to high absenteeism, turnover, and added costs to the employer (Alcer, 2008).

Q6. Did workplace bullying affect your relationship with friends, co-workers, family members, either within and outside your organization? If so, how?

This study's participants dealt with bullying in different ways. While some internalized the stress of bullying and kept it to themselves, others shared their experience with family members—but not always successfully. Some relationships were, at best, surviving due to workplace bullying.

Leonard: *I never discussed it with anyone.*

Debra: *I am a friendly person but am skeptical very much of people because I don't know what their agenda is. They invite other people to certain things sending subtle messages. Very much so, you are more skeptical with people you work with. I call them Cronies. They are relatives, friends, all these people are related. They don't feel that they need to be with others. The organization needs to bring in people who see the big picture. Government is going to work hard to bring people in who reflect their communities.*

Steve: *People you have a close relationship with become more isolated. Sometimes you gain wisdom by discussing things with others. It doesn't generally help those situations where people are more remote. It doesn't help to make those situations better.*

Wayne: *Relationships with co-workers negatively affects home life. You take frustrations out on your family because you can't take it out on your supervisor.*

Charles: *Yes, I did not really look at the bully as a good person. At first I didn't feel this way but after witnessing and experiencing bullying, my perspective changed.*

Phillip: *It changed my whole outlook on how I look at others.*

James: *My attitude, I would bring it home. I always had it on my mind. Did I do this or that right? I went to the gym a lot to relieve stress. At one time, I was drinking beer to relieve stress, but that was only causing more anxiety.*

Leon: *No. It depends on the level of bullying.*

Emily: *I went home and told my husband and he said he didn't want to hear it because he has problems too. I talked to my supervisor talked about my bully co-worker. He stopped and after a while he went back to his old ways. He even bullies my supervisor.*

Mike: *No, because we all related to it. It was long-term employment and the money made working for the schools was good.*

Rick: *I don't take it home to my family once I leave my job.*

While social support from outside the workplace (e.g., family and friend) may help mitigate stress, the bullying may diminish that social support when a victim finds him/herself constantly complaining about their experiences in the workplace. Moreover, WB can directly impact members of the target's family when the victim brings stress and anger home and shifts it to family members. Children, in particular, may be greatly affected. Consider the parent who had had rough day at work sitting at the dinner table relating bullying experiences. Children may feel cowardly, fearful or begin to bully other children at school in frustration. Bullying may also enhance the possibility of marital problems or even domestic violence. Because the target is suffering from anxiety that may lead to stress-related health problems and anger-management issues, the possibility of transference or displacement onto the "innocent bystander" is ever present (Jennifer, Cowie, & Ananiadou, 2003; Rayner et al., 2002; Tracey et al., 2006). However, Jennifer et al. (2003) indicated that emotional withdrawal due to victimization is more common than displacement. For example, a victim returns home from work and is exhausted from emotional abuse. He retires to bed, falls asleep, but finds he has difficulty sleeping. This sleep deficit eventually affects relationships with his family because he may behave irrationally, withdraws from familial interactions, and refuses to participate in activities. In the worst-case scenarios, such withdrawals can lead to separation, divorce, and possible estrangement from children (Jennifer et al., 2003).

In contrast, many say nothing and suffer in silent. Leonard ("I never discussed it with anyone") is one such example. His response ties in with research indicating that targets suffer silently because they may feel no one would believe their stories, they do not know how to explain what is happening, they fear being labeled as a cry baby or a trouble maker, and they're afraid of negative repercussions from reporting WB (Peterson et al., 1995).

Importantly, targets may not be aware of the importance of receiving social support to enhance coping abilities. According to Mikkels (1995), social support and social networks are helpful because:

- Individuals share health information that helps targets identify sources of their health problems
- Friendship networks promote a sense of responsibility toward others.
- Support systems mitigate psychological stress; moreover, the presence of helpful others reduces anxiety.

Louis and Orford (2005) conducted a qualitative study to investigate the role that a collective consciousness may play among organizational members. The ten female participants had all experienced WB and shared their subjective experiences. The authors indicated that a lack of workplace support is concomitant with a decrease in the target's mental resources and ability to defend herself—making her more vulnerable to the bully.

The following question was added to identify any structural contributors to workplace bullying, although not the main focus of this investigation:

Q7. Do you think the organization's culture may have contributed to your bullying experience? If so, how?

The culture and climate of an organization are likely to be consistent throughout all levels; as such, they are reflected in the behavior style of management. Bullying is subtly encouraged and reinforced when the bullying culture persists or the bully's antagonistic behaviors are ignored (Brodsky, 1997). According to Yamada (2000), when bullying is embedded in the culture it can become entrenched at all levels, meaning that the victim has few supportive resources to turn to for help. Some of the participants spoke to this very issue.

Leonard: *Always the case, you have a supervisor and management who know what is going and do nothing about it. That is a blackout for them. The post office has terrible management. You wouldn't believe what goes on. I actually got fired and it is probably the best thing that ever happened to me. Always, core problem is with the organization. Strategic management covers hospital in Virginia. My assignment was to have an interview with Planning and ask if the military can have more nurse aides. The enlisted technicians in the military are doing more. Military training is always geared to get the mission accomplished. That's why technicians can draw blood and prescribe medications. I obtained a management job in the hospital upon graduation didn't know how hospital politics worked. The head nurse, a colonel, hated my guts. I reported directly to the doctors. She felt my services should me under nursing services. She called me into her office one day. She told me to sit down and not say a word. She talked about how badly I was doing. She was trying to railroad me and showed me an incident report I had never seen before about something that happened in the NCO Club. She was mean to everyone and badgered Lt. Nurses so they much they refused to reenlist. There were IG complaints and congressional complaints, but still nothing happened.*

Steve: *Culture is a shared experience. Senior management accepts this behavior. It is what management is used to doing, intimidations, craziness, and all that stuff. Some feel bullying increases productivity. Good companies do not have these problems.*

Emily: *The organization has people who like to bully. I think bullying is embedded in culture. In large organizations people are snitching on others. Some veterans have psychological problems and drug addiction. A lot of them are on medication. The bully has been on a program for drug addiction and is acting better now since his job was threatened.*

Mike: *There was a culture of bullying in the organization. It went through a change when a strong Christian came in as the superintendent. The people then felt more relaxed. My superintendent, no names mentioned [gave me a letter of recommendation and I was promoted within the last 5 years.*

James: *Some of the members of the organization thought they could bully those under them because the CO bullied most of those under her. She was in charge of medical and finance and had only a high school education. It was only because she was hired years ago when the qualifications weren't as high. I tried to get her attention about different problems and got fed up so had to go even higher in the chain of command.*

Rick: *The system tries to keep you down. You are bullied more when you are a good worker. The bully is in a clique and they feel like it strengthens numbers. The bully feels like he has backup and support and the bully provokes situations to cause me to blow up. People talk to you like you are a child or a slave and if you say anything, you will be written up like a second class citizen.*

Leon: *It is harder and harder to find a job. They are jealous which is why they bully. Their way of thinking is too flawed. Your job is most important, but everyone has a breaking point.*

Debra: *Yes, Cronies hire relatives and friends and all have the same mentality. They want to shape people to meet their expectations. Private companies have changed more because of lawsuits. You go in and apply multiple times and you see people getting promoted who don't look* *like you. The culture does need to change. We need people there who reflect their community. There is no tolerance of what they will allow. They need diversity and less bullying. No we shouldn't allow bullying at all. The organization is not inclusive. Overall, I feel every day that they are far from being politically correct. They need to improve the way people are being treated. I don't think they are. When you take a job somewhere, you don't want to get fired. As long as the work is getting done and it doesn't affect productivity, maybe this is their line of thinking. When you are standing up to that person, what are they going to say, did that happen? Who would believe my story? That was the best thing I could do, just get out of there. I said never again, never again. I just want to say, I think this is a worthy research project. In the past the word harassment entailed everything. Bullying is in its own category. Now we have a name for it and a face for it.*

Charles: *Organizations just wanted to get job done and didn't care about the emotional welfare of the employees. Bullying was not intentional. When one person saw it was working, they wanted to try it too. Management doesn't care, management just wants to have the job done. I didn't want to work there anymore and started looking for other jobs.*

Analysis of responses to Question 7. Workplace bullying flourishes for numerous reasons, heightening the need for additional research and expanded knowledge about the phenomenon (Salin, 2003). Additional research should approach workplace bullying as a very strong (but oftentimes secret) invisible network (Hielsin, 2003). Workplace bullying is conceptualized as a form escalated conflict, and researchers emphasize the personality traits of both targeted individuals and perpetrators in explaining how they are prone to assuming these victim/victimizer roles (Zapf & Einarsen, 2003). Management, therefore, can play a role in minimizing interpersonal conflict through policy formulation, educational programming, and HR mediation (Salin, 2003).

According to Rogers and Kelloway (1997), the worker may blame the organization for "allowing" the aggression to occur, compromising the individual's affective bond with the organization. Steve corroborated this viewpoint when he indicated that the organization was to blame for allowing bullying to occur. Archer (1999) found that participants in his study also blamed management for allowing bullying behaviors. He theorized that managers do behave within parameters of the organization's perceived expectations and further pointed out that the organization normalizes certain behaviors. All newcomers in the organization are expected to exhibit these behaviors or face ridicule, bullying, or ostracism. Managers may therefore encourage anti-social behavior which is not condoned, but can be passed off as normal. This is particularly true in highly-disciplined organizations, such as the military, where it is perceived to be part of the nature of the organization.

Additionally, several participants indicated that diversity in the workplace in many cases may have exacerbated workplace bullying. "Because people are generally uncomfortable with differences, they are more likely to attribute hostile motivations to those they perceive as different from them, leading to communication problems, misperception and ultimately, more conflict" (Daniel, 2009, pp. 54).

Workplace Bullying in the Military

Although this investigation canvassed the opinions of individuals who at one time had served in the military, the incidences of bullying described herein largely occurred in the civilian or governmental (non-military) sector. Additionally, the researcher herself is a former military employee. Thus, it is important to include a brief section on bullying in the military, which although has improved to a significant degree, but is not without its problems, particularly in the case of race and gender.

Many might justifiably accuse the military of being the poster-child for workplace bullying in the past. However, significant changes in the structure and membership of the armed forced have significantly changed this perception.

In particular, all branches are now composed of volunteer forces that are better educated about recognizing and reporting bullying. Nonetheless, it is wrong to assume that the military is immune from bullying. The Air Force has even experienced high suicide rates that may be partly due to bullying. Yamada (2015) posited that workplace bullying is no more or less frequent in the military than in other work realms. A survey conducted in 1999 with over 40,000 military personnel found that while many in the military are more comfortable living and working together with all members of their community, 51% said nothing had been done when they made formal complaints about various racial incidents. And more recently, the topic of gender-based cyber-bullying has come to the forefront: "Growing concerns about the online phenomenon parallel heightened awareness of the extent of harassment and assaults on women in uniform and demands by advocates and political supporters for accountability, from perpetrators to top commanders" (Jowers, 2015).

Wayne, who had served in the military, was adamant that "Bullying is not tolerated in the military." In contrast, he later experienced bullying as a civilian—but at the hands of a former Navy employee. James, however, expressed a different view.

> ***James***: I was on a regular maneuver with my troops and the lieutenant. He wanted us to travel in a vehicle that was unsafe. I told him I refused to let my troops board that vehicle. The lieutenant reprimanded me for not following orders. Sometime later, the lieutenant drove the vehicle himself and became involved in a wreck. We went before the company commander, he ended up chewing the lieutenant and not me.

One study participant (Kenneth) recalled a conflict with a military co-worker (a subordinate) because the individual expressed some hostility towards him because of race. In fact, Kenneth admitted that he assigned dirtier jobs to this individual because the chain of command made it easier for him to do so. Rather than take better corrective measures, he used his authority to bully the subordinate. Research indicates that supervisors who perceive themselves as victims of injustices (e.g., racism) from subordinate may be more likely than others to abuse their subordinates (Aryee et al., 2007; Tepper, Duffy, Henle & Lamert, 2006). Accordingly, Kenneth may have felt relatively safe to channel his frustration to a subordinate in retaliatory behavior against a soldier in a defenseless position (Tepper et al., 2006). In contrast, Wayne spoke positively about the intolerance for bullying in the military, which supports recent scholarship. According researchers, there is an increasing trend toward zero tolerance for bullying in the military (Cieslak, 2012; Vergun, 2012). The military services promulgate a decades-old commitment to tolerance and equality among its ranks. Nonetheless, subtle forms of bullying, and particularly gender-based bullying, still occur. The brutal attack to resolve a conflict with a co-worker, as reported by Joseph, would have occurred more frequently in the early 1960s but such attacks are far more rare today. By all accounts the armed services are working hard to ensure that personal character and values are promoted, and that the environment is positive and supportive. But like any organization, there will inevitably be individuals who resort to unsavory tactics to promote their own agenda.

Leymann's Typology of Behaviors

Revisiting Chapter 2, Leymann (1990) posited five behaviors that bullies use to target a coworkers reputation, work performance, communication with co-workers, social circumstances, and threat of or real physical coercions. These behaviors are subdivided into 45 specific behaviors, which are known as Leymann's Inventory of Psychological Terror (LIPT). They are also acts characteristic of mobbing behaviors because they may include multiple perpetrators.

Another goal of this study was to extrapolate the prevalence of the bullying behaviors described in the narratives of this study's 13 participants in terms of the LIPT. Of the five typologies, only four were reported by the respondents, which is why "attacks or threats of real physical coercion" are not included in Table 5.

Table 5

Prevalence of Leymann's Typology of Behaviors Among Study Participants

Typology or Behavior	Never or Rarely (%)	Systematically (%)
ATTACKS ON REPUTATION		
People talk badly behind your back	92.4%	7.6%
Unfounded rumors are circulated	84.62%	15.38%
You are ridiculed	61.54%	38.56%
You are forced to undergo a psychiatric evaluation	92.4%	7.6%
Your private life is ridiculed	84.62%	15.38%
Your nationality is ridiculed	76.92%	23.08%
You are forced to do a job affecting self-esteem	84.62%	15.38%
Efforts are judged as wrong or demeaning	46.15%	**53.85%**
Your decisions are questioned	46.15%	**53.85%**
You are called demeaning names	92.4%	7.6%
ATTACKS ON WORK PERFORMANCE		
Supervisor take away assignments so you cannot even invent new tasks to do	84.62%	15.38%
Corollary damage creates financial costs for you	76.92%	23.08%
Damaging your home or workplace	84.62%	15.38%

Typology or Behavior	Never or Rarely (%)	Systematically (%)
ATTACKS ON COMMUNICATION		
Your supervisor restricts the opportunity for you to express yourself	76.92%	23.08%
You are interrupted constantly	76.92%	23.08%
Colleagues/co-workers restrict your opportunity to express yourself	92.4%	7.6%
You are yelled at and loudly scolded	76.92%	23.08%
Your work is constantly criticized	46.15%	**53.85%**
There is constant criticism about your private life	92.4%	7.6%
Oral threats are made	84.62%	15.38%
Written threats are made	92.4%	7.6%
ATTACKS ON SOCIAL CIRCUMSTANCES		
People do not speak with you anymore	92.4%	7.6%
You cannot talk to anyone (access to others is denied)	92.4%	7.6%
You are put into a workplace that is isolated from others	84.62%	15.38%
You are treated as if you are invisible	92.4%	7.6%

Note: Questionnaire from Leymann (1990)..

The results from this questionnaire reveal that more than half of the respondents (53.85%) said their work was constantly criticized, while 46.15% indicated that their work was rarely or never criticized. Similarly, 53.85% of respondents reported that their efforts were judged as wrong; they were demeaned and their decisions were questioned. This finding supports the theory that attempts to lower a victim's self-esteem may be among the first negative attacks used by bulliers. According to the WBI (2014), approximately 35% of the American workforce (which translates to over 50 million workers) report being the victim of WB; while an additional 15% of workers have witnessed it. When these percentages are totaled we see that half of the American workforce has experienced workplace bullying. These numbers corresponds to the small cohort that took part in this investigation.

Summary

In WB-prone workplaces, management and supervisors tend to be directive and authoritarian, and people often feel that their needs are ignored. Those at the top have prerogative power and may have little interaction with those in lower levels of the organization. When a division of this nature characterizes the culture of the workplace, subordinates at lower levels may feel (justifiably or not) inferior. Moreover, workers may feel disempowered because of bureaucratic structures.

It should be noted too, that bosses may also be bullied by subordinates, For example, a secretary may fail to deliver messages, hide notes, change documents, etc. Such actions are taken to make a supervisor appear incompetent (Hall, 2005). Research finds that similar to downward or lateral bullying (reported by two participants), upward bullying can also lead to stress-related illnesses and anxiety (Hall, 2005).

Adult bullying at the workplace is shockingly common and enormously destructive (Lutgen-Sandvik & Davenport-Sypher, 2009). In taking part in this study, the 13 participants in this study voluntarily shared their experiences and frustrations in order to add to the literature about stopping WB. While only one participant said he was fired from his position, another took an optional retirement option rather than continue to put up with the bullying. Although it is important to note that the WB experiences among these individuals varied widely, it would appear that the remaining 11 apparently had coping abilities that allowed them to hold onto their jobs despite experiencing or witnessing workplace bullying. Nonetheless, it is extremely crucial that the complex issue of WB be more fully explored so that it can be addressed and eradicated from the workplace.

CHAPTER 5.

DISCUSSION, IMPLICATIONS, RECOMMENDATIONS

Discussion

This study was designed to determine how victims of workplace bullying perceived their WB experiences in the context of possible adverse personal and professional outcomes in six areas: physical health, psychological health, self-esteem, interpersonal relationships, job satisfaction/career, and their workplace productivity. Data was obtained inductively based on the voices and experiences of 13 participants in the study. Results from this study are expected to increase awareness of the prevalence of this insidious problem. Because targets are all-too-often unable to stop repetitive negative acts committed against them by perpetrators—usually because of the power disparities that exist between victim(s) and their bully (Keashly & Neuman, 2004)—they may suffer long-term, sometimes permanent psychological and occupational impairments (Crawford, 2001; Leymann & Gustaffson, 1996).

The data was gathered through use of semi-structured telephone interviews between the researcher and the participants who recounted their lived bullying experiences. The interviewees consisted of 13 military veterans, ranging in ages 28-73 and of varying educational achievement levels, ranging from having high school diplomas to one having a doctorate degree. Most had jobs in the civilian labor force, but two were retirees and one served on active duty in the military. The data was coded and assessed by means of analytic induction (Cassell & Symon, 1994; Shanghassy, Zechmeister & Zechmeister, 2000). Five overarching themes emerged from the analysis that corroborate findings from the existing literature on workplace bullying—that it is a highly prevalent and harmful phenomenon (Mikkelson & Einarsen, 2002).

- Stress resulting from workplace bullying can be harmful to one's physical and/or psychological health,
- Workplace bullying can impact a person's self-esteem to the extent that the person begins to engage in self-doubting and self-questioning,
- Stressors in the military environment are antecedents of bullying,
- The organizational culture may be an antecedent of workplace bullying; and
- Workplace bullying has an adverse effect on job satisfaction and productivity.

Discussion of Results in Light of the Literature

Workplace Bullying and its Impact on Physical and Psychological Health

Stress resulting from workplace bullying can be harmful to one's physical and/or psychological health. In this investigation 7 of the 13 respondents (~54%) identified stress from workplace bullying as negatively impacting their physical and psychological health. In extreme cases, two of the participants reported developing physical impairments that required the attention of a physician, surgeon or physical therapist. Debra received physical therapy because of knots in her back and neck that she solely attributes to bullying. James sought medical attention for high blood pressure, which he liked directly to WB. James also had to undergo surgery on his shoulder, which he said was aggravated by WB-related stress. Emily and Mike reported symptoms of stomach problems and headaches due to exposure to workplace bullying, and Rick complained of insomnia from his daily encounters with workplace bullying.

Psychological symptoms included anxiety, tension, and post-traumatic stress disorder (PTSD). Steve reported bullying as generating anxiety and the fright-or-flight reaction when he indicated that "there is stress in observing a stressful environment. It creates anxiety and all that stuff, and a fight-or-flight reaction starts up." Emily and Charles also experienced stress from their WB experiences. James had to consult with professional counselors because of PTSD-like symptoms that he linked to bullying experiences both in the military and in the civilian workplace. Similarly, Charles had to seek treatment from a psychiatrist because of experiences as a Marine veteran and on his current job. He said he was advised "not to take everything so personally," which supports the "blaming-the-victim" literature.

Charles and James were both Vietnam-era veterans. Much of what is known about combat-induced PTSD is has been linked to the American experience in Vietnam, which prompted a thorough assessment of post-traumatic stress as a diagnosable disorder (Wilson, 1980). As noted earlier, Complex-PTSD can result from the accumulation of small, non-life threatening events that are not directly combat-related—such as workplace bullying (Herman, 1997). In situations that could lead to C-PTSD, the victim is under the control of the perpetrator and is trapped or cannot escape the harm or danger due to physical, psychological, maturational, environmental or social constraints (Herman, 1997). Symptoms of C-PTSD include a range of disturbances in self-regulatory capacities (e.g., Ford, Courtois, Steele, Vander Hart, & Nijenhuis, 2005; van der Kolk, Roth, Pelcovitz, Sunday, & Spinazzola, 2005). Hyper-vigilance has also been associated with C-PTSD, which is spurred on by a state of anxiety created in response to external events. In the case of workplace bullying, the triggering event is usually when encountering abusive supervision. Subjects interviewed for this investigation reported developing a heightened sense of vulnerability and difficulty believing what was actually happening to them. Other symptoms include reliving experiences through current dreams or memories, flashbacks, withdrawal from life, becoming overly emotional, and developing a sense of hopelessness (Leymann & Gustafsson, 1996).. James turned to alcohol, which is a coping mechanism associated with both forms of PTSD, and Rick to occasionally smoking marijuana once or twice a week to cope with stress from bullying. Both, however, said this these coping mechanisms only made the problem since it didn't get to the root of the issue. Emily and Mike reported stomach problems brought on by intense stress of having been bullied. Quite often, the long-term physical and emotional strain of WB will lead to burnout (Nielsen & Einarsen, 2012). Such was the case with Debra, who was ready to leave her job rather than face continued incidences of WB. Some targets of workplace bullying become so damaged that they can never reintegrate into the workplace, or can only do so after intensive, specialized treatments and therapies (Leymann & Gustafsson, 1996). Although James was not traumatized to that extent, he did opt for an early retirement for health reasons

According to WBI (2012), nearly three-quarters (71%) of targets of workplace bullying have sought treatment from a physician for psychological or physical care—which was the case for at least two contributor to this study, namely, James and Rick. A person's exposure to the gradual, subtle, and cumulative acts of workplace bullying can overtime result in severe psychological trauma, lowered self-esteem (Randle, 2003), depression, anxiety (Hoel et al., 2003), PTST (Mikkelson et al., 2002), and even suicide (Carbo & Hughes, 2010). Fortunately, this was not the case with any of the 13 participants in this study

Workplace Bullying and Its Effects on Self-Esteem

Self-esteem is enormously important in the workplace. It is a measure of how we value our intrinsic selves, how worthwhile we think we are to others (our extrinsic selves), and how we view our contributions to the world. As such, self-esteem can impact every aspect of our lives—from personal relationships to our work. A person with high self-worth will have the flexibility to deal with adversity and grow from mistakes—and not be fearful of rejection. In contrast, low self-esteem can prevent a person from achieving his/her full potential if that person is plagued with feelings of incompetence, unworthiness, and ineptitude—all of which can further propagate such feelings. Bullying can take a toll on self-esteem when the perpetrator eventually starts chipping away at that confidence. In contrast, generalized feelings of self-efficacy appear to insulate the victim from the psychological impact of bullying (Mikkelsen &

Einarsen, 2002). While individuals with high self-esteem view themselves as competent and successful, those with low self-esteem are more likely to view themselves as failures (Ferris et al., 2008). Persons having low self-esteem may also exhibit signs such as shyness, poor communication skills, depression, and withdrawal.

More than half of this study's cohort reported that bullying had impacted their self-esteem…while five other did not. In general, the victims of bullying who spoke about self-esteem indicated that envy and the presence of a weak, vindictive superior were the most common reasons for bullying. Moreover, among those whose self-esteem appeared to be impacted, constant criticism led to job stress and, in some cases, the belief that they must have been doing something wrong (Landry, 1999). In particular, Debra and Steve both indicated that they began second-guessing themselves or were beginning to develop feelings of self-doubt as a result of constant criticisms. Recall that James admitted incidences when his supervisor would stand over him as if to suggest that he was incompetent, and Emily expressed aggravation in feeling that her supervisor was trying to undermining her capabilities.

Weakened job performance as a result of bullying is consistent with existing literature indicating that exposure to bullying "…manifest itself organizationally, as reduced motivation, creativity, as well as a rise in errors and accidents" (Hoel, et al., 2011, p. 130). Examining the impact of abusive supervision of self-esteem is important because self-esteem is highly correlated with job performance (Judge & Bono, 2001), and poor job performance the leads to organization inefficiency.

Stressors in the Military Environment and Antecedents of Bullying

Even though the military publicizes a policy of zero tolerance for bullying, many job stressors in the military environment such as work pace, job demands, supervisory control, and shift work are comparable to civilian workplace environments (Bogg & Cooper, 1995). The antecedents for WB to occur are therefore also widely prevalent in the military. Compound all the "usual" WB risk factors with the heightened stressors associated with active-duty service—the principal one being the very real risk of death or injury—and that's a possible game-changer (Bogg & Cooper, 1995). Dolan & Ender (2008), for example, reported the results of a study using a sample of 141 participants from service members on active duty. The subjects included both enlisted members and officers. Many of the interviewees in the study perceived the military to be a stressful environment, as evidenced by an enlisted soldier who complained about the relentless pace of work with very little time to recover between missions. Dolan and Ender (2008) added that even though many leaders are genuinely concerned about their welfare of their charges, they can only go so far in extending the hand of kindness. Rightly or wrongly, as an all-volunteer organization the attitude of "This is the Army/Navy/Air Force/ Marines: If you can't take it—get out" is a very real imperative for the safety and welfare of all personnel. Nonetheless, most soldiers in their study blamed poor leadership as a cause of their stress and especially regarding workload and lack of predictability (Dolan & Ender, 2008).

Is there bullying in the military? Of course. Every branch is characterized by significant racial and gender diversity, a top-down management structure, and in many cases high-stress assignments that may separate families and limit support structures. The fact that the military puts such a high priority on zero-tolerance for WB means that it is already miles ahead of far too many private-sector and governmental organizations who are turning a blind eye to the problem.

Organizational Culture as an Antecedent of Workplace Bullying

According to Shehan (1999), bullying behavior is often ignored, tolerated, misinterpreted, or even instigated by the organization's management as a deliberate management strategy. Bullying is further enhanced by externalities in the environment such as a weak economy, poor job markets, negative reports in the media, and the prevailing political climate. Several researchers have asserted that bullying will go unnoticed and underreported in organizations where the culture tolerates and normalizes such behavior (Rhodes, Pullen,

Vickers, Clegg & Pitsis, 2010; Vickers, 2006; Hudson, Roscigno & Lopez, 2006). In contrast, a workplace that actively discourages WB will educate every employee on how to recognize and eliminate the pernicious phenomenon of workplace bullying.

This study revealed that workers generally remain silent about wrongdoing in their organization unless an issue or conflict arises. If a supervisor or member of upper management is investigated, the investigation's results are usually favorable for them. For example, James said when he reported the presence of mice in the cafeteria, he was told to get counseling. It was not until an employee was physically attacked by a mouse that his superiors began taking any action. And recall that Leonard was actively bullied by a female lieutenant colonel appeared to have full immunity from her actions ("There were IG complaints and congressional complains, but still nothing happened").

Cultural norms dictate whether or not bullying is acceptable and/or functional. In fact, if bullying is viewed as functional it may be regarded as an efficient means for accomplishing tasks (Salin, 2003). In some cultures an appearance of toughness is even celebrated (Baron & Neuman, 1977). In Leonard's case, the organization may have chosen to ignore bullying complaints as long as the lieutenant colonel was accomplishing the primary objective. In fact, I would argue that for all of the 13 narratives, each participant's organization tended to have this primary objective in mind. Moreover, no mention was made of any sort of institutional anti-bullying policy—or certainly none that was made known to employees. In every case of WB, the participants either struggled to enhance their coping skills or left the organization entirely—unless there was an eventual change of leadership as with Mike and the school district.

Six of the participants in this study suggested that bullying is both embedded in the culture and reinforced by the organization. Thus, when complaints are filed against the bully, the perpetrator tends to slip through the cracks and is rarely held fully accountable for his/her actions. These bullies may not be highly valued by management, but management typically prefers not to air their dirty laundry in public by admitting to having employed someone who is capable of such harassment.

Thus, in order to stop bullying the culture must be turned upside down. Perpetrators must know that negative consequences await them if they persist in harming others. Promotions must be replaced with justifiable punishments—and senior management must be educated that there is *zero* wiggle room for anyone who engages in such behaviors. As noted earlier, however, since executives tend to be the bully's best friends and supporters, it is a difficult change to embed in the culture of an organization.

Workplace Bullying and Its Effects on Job Satisfaction and Productivity

The consequences for workplace bullying can be severe for both employees and employers. The costs for employers from such factors as reduced efficiency and productivity, increased absenteeism, staff turnover, increased costs for recruitment and training, adverse publicity, and skyrocketing legal costs for defending a worker's compensation claim (and others) mean that bullying is both damaging for the employee and expensive for the organization.

This study confirmed that workplace bullying from hindrance stressors (Cavanaugh et al., 2000) leads to job dissatisfaction and possible job change. Among participants in this study, (a) Debra left her place of employment after finally admitting to herself that her health was more important than her job, (b) Wayne and Emily were both considering leaving their jobs, (c) Steve changed companies, (d) Leonard was fired (happily for him), and (e) James took an early retirement. When such options were not possible due to financial reasons, victims sought advice and engaged in coping mechanisms—some of a negative nature such as drinking. James, however, said he met with a psychologist, who suggested that he change his mindset as a form of "therapy." In situations where the aggression cannot be prevented, other avenues for reducing the risk of low productivity and dissatisfaction include psychosocial workplace interventions, stress management training, relaxation, meditation, and coping skills training (La Montague, Kegel, Louicl, Ostgry, & Lansbergis, 2007).

Bullying in the workplace occurs as often as it does because the acts are not recognized as harassment and are therefore ignored (Einarsen, 1999). Moreover, organizations may purposively choose to ignore or minimize them in order to preserve the "productivity status quo" unless they are mandated to do otherwise (McLaughlin, 2014; White, 2004).

Implications of Workplace Bullying

According to Nielsen & Einarsen (2012), empirical studies over the past three decades has established workplace bullying as an important social problem that has devastating effects for those bullied, those exposed to bullying, the organization, and society at large. Findings show that the primary implications of workplace bullying is that it leads to mental and physical health problems, symptoms of PTSD, burnout, increased intention of victims and bystanders to leave, and reduced job satisfaction and organizational commitment (Nielsen & Einarsen, 2012).

Workplace bullying is pervasive across all types of organizations; in fact, the estimated global prevalence rate for WB is now 11%-18% depending on the measurement method used (Nielsen & Einarsen, 2012). With studies that showing that over 54 million persons are affected by workplace bullying each year (Nielsen & Einarsen, 2012), it has become a major challenge for organizations to recognize and eliminate it. Because there are relatively few theories to guide workplace-bullying research—say, for example, in comparison to studies of harassment—it is more difficult to quantify and examine the phenomenon (Hogh et al., 2011).

At the grassroots level, most workers are unaware of the dynamics and patterns of WB largely because it typically involves covert acts that can gradually escalate. In other worse, it can creep into an organization's culture with little or no pushback. According to researchers, there is no single reason why people bully, but the phenomenon is known to include both organizational and individual factors (Salin, 2003; Skogstad, Matthiesen & Einarsen, 2007; Zapf & Einarsen, 2003).

As indicated above, the negative effects from WB are heightened when it develops into repeated and *chronic cognitive activation* (Nielsen & Einarsen, 2012), which, in essence, means that the victim comes to expect to be bullied. Chronic cognitive activation over an extended period of time often leads to a variety of physical and mental health impairments, as detailed earlier (Ursin & Eriksen, 2004). Of particular importance is the link between bullying, PTSD, and burnout, which can occur over many years due to stress and the inability to reach personal goals Nielsen & Einarsen (2012). PTSD and workplace burnout are known precursors for exhaustion and occupational detachment and reduced productivity (Nielsen & Einarsen, (2012). Sufferers also complain of job dissatisfaction, fatigue, and impaired cognitive performance (Schmidt, Neubach & Heuer, 2007). Longitudinal studies of victims treated for WB-related burnout show that even though many were able to return to their jobs, symptoms continued to persist (Blonk, Brenninkmeijer, Lagerveld & Houtman, 2006).

Many organizations deny that there is bullying in their organizations and instead choose to bury their organizational head in the sand. This reality explains why some participants found it useless to address management with this issue. As Charles pointed out, "Nothing would have been done about it anyway." Management tends to be more concerned about the bottom line financially than with addressing WB—which is interesting since bullying is known to be costly to an organization. Even worse, Archer's (1999) study of bullying among firefighters indicated that organizations sometimes encourage the behavior when the bully is identified as a strong manager who knows how to get things done.

In revisiting Chapter 2, this study confirms that organizations are quick to deny bullying because (a) it reflects badly on management, and (b) it may mean unwanted changes to a deeply-entrenched organizational culture that promulgates such insidiousness. Accordingly, most of the participants felt it would be fruitless to complain to management. This finding reinforces that organizational power dynamics play a role in workplace bullying (Hutchinson, Vickers, Jackson, & Wilkes, 2010).

"The implications of workplace bullying can be substantial for management and the effective management of today's employee" (Hall & Lewis, 2010, p. 129). It is no longer limited to unwanted verbal communications, but includes written communication from e-mails, text-messaging and other forms of social media. Currently, no laws have been enacted to protect workers who face cyber-bullying or other "modern" forms of WB. In fact, according to workplaybullying.org, bullying is legal in every U.S. state. Thus, the structural challenges are many, but the stakes couldn't be higher for the health and welfare of the American worker.

Recommendations for Future Research

Several areas warrant further investigation. First, more scrutiny should be paid to delayed injuries from workplace bullying. In other words, a worker may leave a bullying job situation, but continue displaying symptoms of the trauma (or develop new ones) long after he or she has resigned, been terminated, or retired. Thus, more longitudinal research is needed to investigate the linkage between workplace bullying and PTSD or C-PTSD. Further, more research should explore if and how WB may lead to severe trauma. My research revealed that while some respondents indicated that they experienced psychological harm from bullying, others said it had no effect on them at all. But given the complexity of the outcomes, there is a question as to whether the victim is aware of negative psychological consequences or is denying them.

More research is needed to explore the hierarchy of workplace bullying. Does the school bully automatically become the workplace bully? Additionally, when the victim brings his/her WB problems home for support, will a child who is agitated about a parent's workplace bullying experience model that very behavior at school? Additionally, further research must be undertaken to reveal how abusive supervision affects individual performance (Schat & Frone,

2011). According to Conner et Douglas (2005) "… studies need to explore how organizational structures foster stress and how employee predispositions toward structural alternatives can influence the extent these stressors result in increased employee strain (p. 210)."

Zellars, Tepper and Duffy (2002) reported that subordinate's exposure to abusive supervision "… predicted reduced contextual performance via perceptions and procedural injustice (p. 24)." Most research has focused on ill-health as an outcome of work-related stressors; however, studies clearly show the need for additional research examining how stress affects work performance and other behaviors. For example, tension and frustration resulting from stress can escalate bullying in the workplace (Hoel & Salin, 2003).

Additionally, scholars should develop models of leadership that are better equipped to address problems in the modern workplace, which arise, in part, from an increasingly multicultural workforce (Lynham, 1998). Thus, organizational leaders need to acquire knowledge and skills needed to address relational issues that emerge from a diverse workforce and disseminate those throughout the organization (Byrd, 2007).

Bullying researchers need to engage in more studies examining detailed conceptions of power. The fact that so few researchers have explored these conceptions is unfortunate since management structures in the in the workplace continue to change as new models of doing business emerge. This study also revealed insufficient literature on WB from the perspective of the bully. When someone is accused of workplace bullying, how should an organization respond that is least damaging to all parties (e.g., research shows that accusations of bullying have led to suicide)? To date, few researchers have examined the impact on people accused of bullying, which appear to be serious (Jenkins, Zapf, Winefield & Sauis, 2012). The problem is complex as summarized by Jenkins et al. (2012): "Managers who are accused of bullying may believe they are struggling against a recalcitrant worker's resistance to necessary change. On the other hand, workers may consider their aggressive actions to be legitimate attempts to protect their employee rights" (p. 5).

A final recommendation for further research involves investigating impaired cognitive functioning for sufferers of WB-related burnout. The literature states that current cognitive behavioral therapies are ineffective in restoring the cognition of sufferers to "normal" levels. Indeed, it would appear that relatively little is known about the course of the symptoms and impaired cognitive performance (van Dam, Keijsers, Eling, & Becker, 2012).

Assumptions Revisited

The first assumption was participants suffered as a direct result of experiencing or exposure to workplace bullying. It was also assumed the researcher's findings would be based on correct interpretations which would promote interests in developing meanings from the responses of participations. This assumption was corroborated when participants recalled the bully's persistent efforts to lower their self-esteem and cause them to develop a sense of disempowerment—both of which created higher than normal anxiety levels (Salin, 2003). It should be noted that although Charles specifically indicated increased levels of anxiety, other participants did not explicitly mention that. Nonetheless, one cannot claim that WB had no impacts of that nature. Consider Leon, for example, who used physical force against a co-worker bully, which could have been a by-product of heightened levels of anxiety. However, the fact that the researcher captured a mere snapshot of the experiences of participants means that one cannot say for certain. In other words, the degree of suffering varied with each participant and each had developed his or her own coping mechanisms. Leonard turned his bullying situation into a positive job change. In contrast, two participants reporting the development of physical ailments. Again, their abilities to cope often depended on the type and intensity of the stimulus, their own perceptions of the incidents, and its duration. According to Nielsen & Einarsen (2012), "the severity of outcomes of workplace bullying is dependent upon the interaction between the severity and nature of the bullying behaviors, individual characteristics, and coping mechanisms (p. 313).

Another assumption to revisit is that most stressors in the military mirror those in the other workplace environments—for example, having to do with long hours, shift work, and job pace (Bogg & Cooper, 1995). However, there are stressors in the military that are quite different. The risk of injury or death produces a heightened level of stress. Additionally, the culture of the military (as well as other para-military organizations and health services organizations) is more characterized by a strongly structured and power-based culture. (Archer, 1999). Because these organizations are heavily dependent on socialization processes, acceptance, normalization, indoctrination and preservation of hierarchy, bullying is highly influential and potentially the most dangerous (Archer, 1999). Because they are hybrids of power and role, frustrations develop among those who cannot cope with either the lack of opportunities or the nature of their roles (Archer, 1999). Thus, these organizations should be examined separately in terms of the nature of WB and its possible remedies.

Limitations Revisited

First, this study was limited by its small sample size and the fact that these participants (as military veterans) may consciously or unconsciously have held specific views about the nature of bullying due to their prior military experiences. Second, the study did not account for gender differences, ethnic differences, personality styles or any other individualized differences that may have influenced their responses to bullying. Indeed, a study with such a relatively small cohort would have negated any potentially statistically-significant variations based on these factors. Third, it is important to note that this study's findings are limited in that it did not include the perspectives of the perpetrators of WB. In short, "the other side of the story" remains unknowable and limits the generalizability of findings. Similarly, research revealing how victims may consciously or unconsciously contribute to bullying are limited; while this caution may harken back to "blaming the victim," the fact remains that this study describes experiential data that is filtered through time and memory. Rayner (1999) suggested that victims tend to see themselves as blameless and often do not understand how their actions may contribute to bullying. Similarly, Barllen, Neyune, De Witte and DeCuyper (2009) cautioned that "…focusing on only one aspect of the process does not give an accurate explanation of why bullying occurs (p. 11).

Another anticipated limitation of this investigation was the amount of information participants were willing to disclose and/or their candor in doing so. For example, Mike did not want elaborate on bullying incidents in the school district. Similarly, Joseph only disclosed a bullying incident with a co-worker—but as a veteran neither he nor Wayne were willing to talk about analogous incidents in the military, presumably because they didn't want to appear too critical. Some of their hesitancy may also have stemmed from their unwillingness to recall certain experiences. According to Wegner (1997), thoughts or memories that portend negative emotion can consciously or unconsciously be suppressed—which does not mean that they have no power over the individual. Indeed, these thoughts may still be influencing their behavior even if inaccessible (Wenger & Smart, 1997). Participants may also have withheld information for fear of being identified and subsequently reprimanded. Although none of the participants expressed organizational disloyalty or directly blamed the organization, a few expressed concern for what may have been management's condoning of workplace bullying.

Finally, this qualitative study captured the opinions of the 13 participants at a moment in time. Given time limitations, it was not possible to conduct a longitudinal study to discover the long-term affects of workplace bullying, if any. While the participants did not appear to have problems processing any cognitive information as a result of their experiences, it does not mean that they would not experience that or other stress-related conditions in the future.

Conclusions

Bullying is a pervasive problem that appears to be embedded in the culture of the workplace. When allowed to occur, it can result in a variety of physical and psychological problems that can hinder work performance and impact relationships. If and when victims finally decide to confront the problem, they are unlikely to feel supported by management, who may be knowingly or unknowingly protecting the perpetrator in order to maintain organizational productivity and the reputation of the company. Moreover, many victims are reluctant to expose the problem because it could jeopardize their job security, well-being, and possibly exacerbate the problem. Bullying flourishes largely due to fears and misperceptions—and because victims often do not know where to turn to for help. Indeed, organizations such as the Employee Advisory Program tend to be overlooked by victims altogether. As such, these organizations need to reexamine their roles and develop holistic strategies to meet the challenges of stressful, bully-prone work environments.

Mc Laughlin (2014) suggested several tactics that HR can do to help reduce bullying in the workplace: (1) Make the business care about eliminating bullying at all levels of the organization, (2) create and disseminate an unambiguous anti-bullying policy and enhance communication throughout its various units and divisions, (3) hold awareness trainings for employees, (4) establish a neutral, trusted contact for reporting bullying complaints, (5) promptly address any complaints, and (6) provide psychological counseling by professionals trained to recognize and treat victims of WB. The absence of legal statutes against workplace bullying should not mean that organizations are free to ignore the issue.

Research is still lacking as to why the problem persists, despite attempts to "mandate civility" within organizations. It is suggested that exploring less obvious forms of power within organizations could enhance both our understanding of the problem and our ability to influence organizational practices (Fletcher, 1992). Salin (2003) noted that those who have the power to bully are often those who have the power to construct, define and manage bullying. Salin (2003) further noted that when "members of organizations internalize such norms it can then lead to unquestioned compliance with organizational practices, even though they might be discriminatory or disadvantage certain groups" (Salin, 2003. p. 50).

Organizations need to implement policies eliminating workplace bullying and ensure that all workers are familiar with them. When bullying is reported, it should receive immediate attention from management and any guilty party should be held accountable. Additionally, healthcare and legal systems need to be made aware of the possible extreme consequences of workplace bullying. Knowing the signs and symptoms of WB (e.g., stress-related/PTSD-like symptoms) may make victims more likely to report the problem and seek help before it causes lasing physical or psychological harm (Saunders, 1994).

The Healthy Workplace Bill has been proposed as a solution to workplace bullying in the US. Figure 3 lists the plusses and minuses of the bill, which has been introduced in 29 states and 2 territories. Overall, it suffers from the same problems as the current harassment laws and Intentional Infliction of Emotional Distress laws (IIED) laws in this country—namely, the standards are set too high to hold the bully accountable for harm done, and the target is burdened with too many reporting requirement. Clearly, this country has a long way to go to strengthen the legislation against a growing problem (Carbo, 2009).

Potential Positive Outcomes	**Potential Negative Outcomes**
1. Bullying targets have genuine legal claim	1. HWD is used a workplace civility code with too many frivolous claims brought
2. Reduction in bullying behaviors to the benefit of employers and employees alike	2. HWD is unidentified due to judicial rulings and the difficulty of proving a case
3. Liability exposure encourages employers to educate workers, take preventive measures, act responsively	
4. Presence of legal protection serves to heighten public awareness about cost	

Figure 4: Potential Outcomes of Enacting Workplace Bullying Legislation in the Form of The Healthy Workplace Bill.

Figure adapted from Yamada (2015). Retrieved from workplacebullying. org.with permission.

The harmful of effects of bullying may be summed up with a statement by Daniel K. Garitian, from his book, *Stones and Sticks: A Story about Bullying:* "Physically we can heal, but the emotional damage of words and actions can last a lifetime, an injury so deep and painful that it can change someone for the rest of their life, an injury that can steal life from someone, an injury that can drive someone to take their own life."

REFERENCES

ABC Antibullying Crusader (2008). "Stop workplace bullying! Testimony by AntiBullyingCrusador (ABC), Provided at Connecticut State Senate Hearing 02/26/08. Retrieved from www.antibullying crusader wordpress.com/2008.

Adams, A. (1992). *Bullying at work: how to confront and overcome it.* London: Virago.

Adler, P.A. & Adler, P. (1994). Observational techniques: In Denzin, N.K. & Lincoln, Y.S. (Eds.). *Handbook of Qualitative Research.* Thousand Oaks, CA: Sage.

Altheide, D. L., & Johnson, J. M. (1994). Criteria for assessing interpretive validity in qualitative research. In N. K. Denzin & Y. S. Lincoln (Eds.), *Handbook of Qualitative Research* (pp. 485-499). Thousand Oaks, CA: Sage.

Archer, D. (1999). Exploring workplace bullying culture in para-military organizations. *International Journal of Manpower, 20*(1/2). Retrieved from http://www.proquest.com.library.capella.edu.

Aryee, S., Chen, Z.K., Sun, L., & Deborah, Y.A. (2007). Antecedents and outcomes of abusive supervision: Test of a trickle-down model. *Journal of Applied Psychology, 92*, 191-201. doi:10.111/j.1936-4490.1997.

Ashkanasy, N.M. (2003). Emotions in organizations: A multi-level perspective, in Fred Dansereau, Francis J. Yammarino (ed.) *Multi-Level Issues in Organizational Behavior and Strategy (Research in Multi Level Issues, Volume 2)* Emerald Group Publishing Limited, pp. 9 – 54.

Atkins, P.A. (1995). *Qualitative research methods*. London, England: Sage.

Ayoko, O. B., Callan, V.J., & Hartel, C.E.J. (2003). Workplace conflict, bullying, and counterproductive behaviors. *International Journal of Organizational Analysis, 2,* 283-301. Retrieved from EBSCO.com. library.capella.edu.

Badzmierowski, W. (2005). Dealing with office bullies, developing respect, service and safety on the job, *EAP Digest,* Fall, 2005. Baldwin, D.C. (1992). Medical student abuse, *Journal of Organizational and Leadership Studies, 8*(4), 1-16.

Balshem, M. (1988). 'The clerical worker's' boss: An agent of job stress, *Human Organization, 47,* 361-367. doi:10.1002/casp.977.

Bandura, A. (1977). *Social learning theory*. Englewood Cliffs, NJ: Prentice-Hall.

Bandura, A. (1994). Self-efficacy. In V. Roma-Chaudran, *Encyclopedia of Human Behavior* (pp. 71-81) San Diego, CA: Sage.

Bandura A., & Walters, R.H. (1963). *Social learning and personality development*. New York: Holt, Rinehart, and Winston.

Barker, M., Sheehan, M., & Rayner, C. (1999). Introduction: Workplace bullying: Perspectives on a management challenge, *International Journal of Manpower, 20*(1-2), 8-9. Retrieved from http;//www. proquest.com.library.edu.

Baron, R., & Neuman, J.H. (1998). Workplace aggression-the ice beneath the tip of workplace violence: Evidence on its forms, frequency and targets. *Public Administration Quarterly, 21*(4), 446-464.

Bassman, E. (1992). *Abuse in the workplace*. Quorum: New York, NY.

Beasley, J., Rayner, C. (1997). Bullying in adult life. *Journal of Community and Applied Social Psychology,* 7(3), 173-256. doi:10.1298/199706/739.253C177.AID-CASP415%.

Beck, A., Rush, J., Shaw, B., & Emergy, G. (1979). *Cognitive theory of depression (the Guilford clinical psychology and psychopathology series.* New York, NY: Guilford.

Bentz, V.M. & Shapiro, J.J. (1998). *Mindful inquiry in social research, 1ˢᵗ edition.* Sage Publications, Inc.

Bies, R.J. & Tripp, T. M. (2005). The study of revenge in the workplace: Conceptual, ideological, and empirical issues. In S. Fox and P.E. Spector (Eds.), *Counterproductive Work Behavior: Investigations of Actors and Targets.* pp. 61, Washington, DC: American Psychological Association.

Blackwood, K. & Bentley, T. (2013). Out of step? The efficacy of Trans-Tasman law to combat workplace bullying. *Journal of Employment Relations,* pp. 27-41. doi:107617092.

Blonk, R., Brenninkmeijer, V., Lagerveld, S.E., & Houtman, I. (2006). Return to work: A companion of two cognitive behavioral interventions in cases of work-related psychological complaints among the self-employed. *Work and Stress, 20,* 129-144. doi:10.1080/02678370600886615.

Bogg, J. and Cooper, C. (1995). Job satisfaction, mental health, and occupational stress among senior civil servants, *Human Relations, 48,* 327-341.

Bogdon, R. C., & Biklen, S. K. (1982). *Qualitative research for education: An introduction to the theory and methods.* Boston, MA: Allyr and Bacon.

Bjorklund, R. (2004). *Experimental approach to cognitive abnormality among victims of bullying at work.* Proceedings from the Fourth International Conference on Bullying and Harassment in the Workplace, Bergen,

Norway, June. pp. 28-31. Retrieved from http://bora.uib.no/bitstream/handle/1956/2383/Proceedings_BBRG_2004.pdf?sequence=1.

Bosworth, K. & Judkins M. (2014). *Tapping into the power of school climate to prevent bullying: One application of schoolwide positive behavior interventions and supports.* Theory into Practice, 53(4), 300-307. doi:1 0.1080/00405841.2014.947224

Brodsky, C. (1976). *The harassed worker.* Lanham, MD: Lexington Books.

Brown, D.C. (1996). Why ask why patterns and themes of causal attribution in the workplace. *Journal of Industrial Teacher Education, 33*(4), 47-65. Retrieved from scholar.lib.vt.edu/ejournal/JITE/v33n4-Brown.html.

Bully-Free Workplace Website (2008). [online]. Retrieved from hhttp://www.bullyfreeworkplace.org.

Burgess, G., (2014). Bullying in the workplace, [online], Retrieved from https://prezi.com/gafg2r_1zelk/bullying-in-the-workplace/.

Byrd, M. (2007). Educating and developing leaders of racially diverse organizations. *Human Resource Development Quarterly, 18*(2), 275-279. doi:10.1002/hrdq.1203.

Byrne, M.M. (2001). Linking philosophy, methodology, and methods in qualitative research. *AORN Journal, 73*, 207-210. doi:http://dx.doi.org/10.1016/S0001-2092(06)62088-7

Cameron, K. S. & Ettington, D.R. (1988). The conceptual foundations of organizational culture. In Smart, J. C. (Eds.). Higher Education: *Handbook of Theory and Research, 4.* New York, NY: Agatho Press.

Cameron, M.E., Schaffer, M., & Park, H.A. (2001). Nursing student's experiences of ethical problems and use of decision-making models, *Nursing Ethics, 8*, 432. doi:10.1177/096973300100800507

Capella.edu. Informed Consent form. Retrieved from http://blogs.capella.edu/theirb/files/2008/08 template-Informed-consent-pdf.

Carbo, J. (2009). Strengthening the healthy workplace act: Lessons from Title VII and the IIED litigation and stories of targets' experiences. *Journal of Workplace Rights, 14*(1), 97-120. doi:10.2190/WR.14.1.f

Carbo, J. & Hughes, A. (2010). Workplace bullying: Developing a human rights definition from the perspective of experiences of targets. *The Journal of Labor and Society, 13*(3), 387-403. doi:10.1111/j.1743-4580 2010.00297xpdf.

Cassell, C. & Symon G. (1994). *Essential guide to qualitative methods in organizational research.* Thousand Oaks, CA: Sage Publications.

Cavanaugh, M. A., Boswell, W. R., Roehling, M.V., & Boudreau, J. W. (2000). An empirical examination of self-reported work stress among US managers. *Journal of Applied Psychology, 85*(1), 65-74.

Charmaz, K. (1995). Grounded theory. In J.A. Smith, R. Harre, & L. Van Langenhove (Eds.), *Rethinking Methods in Psychology* (pp. 27-49) Thousand Oaks, CA: Sage Publications.

Charmaz, K (2006). *Constructing grounded theory: A practical guide through qualitative analysis (Introducing Qualitative Methods series).* Thousand Oaks, CA: Sage Publications.

Chao, G., Koylowski, S., Smith, E., & Hedlund, J. (1993). Organizational downsizing: Strategies interventions and research implications. *International Review of Industrial and Organizational Psychology, 8*, 263-332.

Chell, E. (2003*). The critical incident technique,* in M. Lewis-Beck, A. Bryman & T. Futing Liao (eds.), The Encyclopedia of Research Methods in the Social Sciences, Thousand Oaks, CA; Sage.

Cooper, C. & Hoel, H. (2000, November). *Destructive conflict and bullying at work*. Extracts of study report compiled for launch of the Civil Service Race Equality Network, Manchester School of Management. Retrieved from www.workplacebullying.org/us/umist.pdf.

Cooper, C.L. & Marshall, J., (1976). Occupational sources of stress: A review of literature relating to coronary heart disease and mental ill-health. *Journal of Occupational Psychology, 49,* 11-28. doi:10.1111/j.2044.8325.1976. tb00325x.

Cooper, C.L., Hoel, H. & Faragher, B. (2001). The experience of bullying in Great Britain: The impact of organizational status. *European Journal of Work and Organizational, 10*(4*),* 443-465.

Cooper, C.L., Hoel, H., & Faragher, B. (2004). Bullying is detrimental to health, but all bullying behaviors are not necessarily equally damaging. *British Journal of Guidance and Counselling, 33,* 367-387. doi:10.108 0/0306988010001723594.

Cowie, H., Naylor, P., Rivers, I., Smith, P.K. & Pereira, B. (2002). Measuring workplace bullying. *Bullying, Aggression, and Violent Behavior, 33-* 51. doi:10.1016/S1359-1789(00)00034-3

Crawford, N. (2001). Organizational responses to workplace bullying. In N. Tehrani (Ed.), *Building a Culture of Respect: Managing Bullying at Work* (pp. 21-31). London, England: Taylor & Francis.

Crenshaw, L. (2008). Taming the abrasive manager: words from the boss whisperer. Retrieved from www.cio.com/article/175650/Taming_the_ Abrasive_Manager_Words_from-The Boss Whisperer.

Creswell, J.W. (2006). *Qualitative inquiry and research design: Choosing among five approaches* (2nd edition), Thousand Oaks, CA: Sage Publications, Inc.

Dade J.M. & Schuering, E.R. (2014). States continue to propose antibullying legislation but fail to act. *Employment Relations Today*, *41*(3), 61-70. doi:10.1002/ert.21466

Dalton, D. (1997) Contemporary research on absence from work: correlates, causes and consequences. In C.L. Cooper and I.T. Robertson (Eds.), *International Review of Industrial and Organizational Psychology* (pp. 115-173). Chichester, UK: John Wiley and Sons.

Daniel, T.A. (2009). *Tough boss or workplace bully? A grounded theory study of insights from human resource professionals,* (Doctoral Dissertation) Retrieved from Proquest.com.library.capella.edu. (UMI No. 350585).

Davenport, N., Schwartz, R.D.Y & Eliott, G.P. (1999). *Mobbing: Emotional abuse in the American workplace*. Amer, Iowa: Civil Society.

Davis, P. (1989) Microaggressions and microinequities: Law as microaggression, *The Yale Law Journal 98,* 1559-1577.

Devlin, B. (2001, April). *Online learning challenges for students using case studies, collaboration, problem-based approaches and role-play simulations*. Paper presented at Flexible Learning Workshops, Charles Darwin University, Darwin, NT, Australia.

Denison, D.R. (1990). *Corporate culture and organizational effectiveness.* New York, NY: John Wiley & Sons.

Dienesch, R. M. and Liden, R.C. (1986). Leader-member exchange model of leadership: A critique further development, *Academy of Management Review, 11*(3), 618-634.

Dilts-Harryman, S. (2007). *Lives reshaped: A heuristic study of workplace bullied targets*, (Doctoral dissertation). Retrieved from http:search. proquest.com.library.capella.edu. (UMI No. 3283779).

Dolan, C. A. & Ender, M.G. (2008). The coping paradox: Work, stress, and coping in the U.S. Army. *Military Psychology*, *20*(3), 151-169. http://dx.doi.org/10.1080/08995600802115987

Douglas, E. (2001) *Bullying in the workplace: An organizational toolkit* (6th edition). London, England: Gower Publishing Ltd.

Dubois, C. L.Z., Faley, R.H . Kustis, G.A. & Knapp, D.E. (1999). Perceptions of organizational responses to formal sexual harassment complaints. *Journal of Management Issues. 11*(2), 198-212.

Duffy, M., Ganster, D., & Pagon, M. (2002). Social undermining in the workplace. *Academy of Management Journal, 45*(2), 331-351. doi:10.2307/3069350

Earnshaw, J. & Morrison, L. (2001). Should employers worry? Workplace stress claims following the John Walker decision. *Personnel Review, 30*(4), 468-487. doi:10.1108/00483480110396339.

Einarsen, S. (2000). Harassment and bullying at work: A review of the Scandinavian approach. *Aggression and Violent Be*havior: *4*(5), 379-401. doi:10.1016/51359-1789(98)00043-3.

Einarsen, S. (2005). The nature, causes, and consequences of bullying at work: The Norwegian experiences. *Pistes, 7,3*. doi:11.1108/014377299910268588.

Einarsen, S., Raknes, B.I., & Matthiesen, S (1994). Bullying and harassment at work and their relationships to work environment quality; an exploratory study. *European Work & Organizational Psychology, 4*(4), 381-401. doi:10.1080/13594 329408410497.

Einarsen, S., & Raknes, B. I. (1991). *Mobbing in work life: A study on prevalence and health effects of mobbing in Norwegian workplaces.* Bergen, Norway: Forksning Center for arbeidsmiljo (FAHS).

Einarsen, S., Raknes, B.I., Mathiesen, S. (1994). Bullying and harassment at work and their relationships to work environment quality: An exploratory study. *European Work and Organizational Psychologist, 4*(4), 381-401. doi:10.1080/14594329408410497.

Einarsen, S., Matthiesen, S. B. & Skogstad, A. (1998). Bullying, well-being, burnout & well-being among assistant nurses. *Journal of Health and Safety-Australia and New Zealand, 14*, 563-568.

Eliason, M. J. (1998) Correlates of prejudice in nursing students, *Journal of Nursing Education, 37*(1), 27-29.

Everton, W.J., Jolton, J.A., & Mastrangelo, P.M. (2007). Be nice and fair or else: Understanding reasons for employee's deviant behaviors. *Journal of Management Development, 26*, 2. doi:10.1108/02621710710726035.

Ferris, D. L., Brown, D.J. Berry, J. W. & Lian, H. (2008). The development and validation of the workplace ostracism scale: *Journal of Applied Psychology, 93*, 1348-1366.

Ferris, P. (2004). A personal view: a preliminary typology of organizational response to Allegations of workplace bullying: see no evil, hear no evil, speak no evil. *British Journal of Guidance and Counseling, 32*, 3. doi: 10.1080/03069880410001723576.

Festinger, L. (1957). *A theory of cognitive dissonance.* Standard, CA: Stanford University Press.

Field, T. (1996). *Bully in sight, how to predict, resist, challenge and combat workplace bullying.* Oxfordshire, England: Success Unlimited.

Field, T. (2003). *Workplace bullying, the silent epidemic.* UK: BMJ Publishing Group.

Fisher-Blando, L.J. (2008). *Workplace bullying, aggressive behavior and its effect on job satisfaction and productivity* (Doctoral dissertation). Retrieved from https://campus.capella.edu.web/library/articles-books-more/databases.

Flanagan, J. C. (1954). The critical incident technique. *Psychological Bulletin, 51,4.*Retrieved http://www.proquest.com.library.capella.edu.

Ford, J., Courtois, C., Steele, K., Vander Hart, D., Nijenhuis, E. (2005). Treatment of Treatment of complex posttraumatic self-dysregulation, *Journal of Traumatic Stress,* 18, 437-447. doi:10, 1002/jts.20051.

Fox, S. & Stallworth, L. (2005). Racial/ethnic bullying: exploring links between bullying and racism in the US workplace, *Journal of Vocational Behavior, 66*(2), 438-456. doi:10.101b/jgvb.2004.01.002.

Garofalo, J. (1986). *Reassessing the lifestyle model of criminal victimization.* In M. Gottfredson and T. Hirschi (eds.) Positive Criminology, Sage, Beverly Hills, CA. pp. 23-42.

Gardner, S. & Johnson, P. (2001). The leaner, meaner workplace: strategies for handling bullies at work. *Employment Relations Today, 28*(2), 23-36. doi:10.1002/ect,1012.

Glendinning, P. M. (2001). Workplace bullying: curing the cancer of the American workplace. *Public Personnel Management, 30*(3), 269-286. Retrieved from http://www.proquest.com.library.capella.edu.

Glomb, T. & Lisa H. (2003). Interpersonal aggression in work groups: social influence, reciprocal and individual effects: *Academy of Management Journal, 46*(4), 486-495. doi:10.2307/30030640.

Glomb, T. M., & Miner, A. G. (2002). Exploring patterns of aggressive behaviors in organizations: Assessing model-data fit. In J.M. Brett & F. Drayou (Eds.). *The psychology of work, theoretically based empirical research* (pp. 235-338), Hillsdale, NJ: Eribaum.

Goffman, E. (1959). *The presentation of self in everyday life.* Garden City, NY:Double Day.

Graen, G., & Uhl-Bien, M. (1995). Relationships based approach to leadership: Development of leader-member exchange (LMX) theory of leadership over 25 years: Applying a multi-level, multi-domain perspective, *Leadership Quarterly,* 6, 219-247. doi:10.1.1.369.1391.

Griffiths, D. (1981). *Psychology and medicine.* London, England: Macmillan.

Groblinghloff, D. & Becker, M. (1996). A case study of mobbing and the clinical treatment of mobbing victims. *European Journal of Work and Organizational Psychology, 5, 2.* doi:10,1080/13594329608414859.

Guba, E.G. (1978). *Toward a methodology of naturalistic inquiry in educational evaluation. Monograph 8.* Los Angeles: UCLA Center of the Study of Evaluation.

Hall, R., & Lewis, S. (2010). Electronic harassment, recruiters, sources, and global benefits. *Human Resources Magazine, 55,* 24-25.

Hammersley, M. & Atkinson, P. (1995). *Ethnography: principles in practice.* New York, NY: Routledge.

Harbison, G. (2004). Employee rights pose lawsuit threat. Retrieved from www.epmag.com/archives/Management report/2435htm.

Harris, K. J., Harvey, P. & Kacmar, K.M. (2011). Abusive supervisory reactions to co-Worker Relationship conflict. *The Leadership Quarterly*, 22(5), 100-1023, http://doi.org/10.1016/j.leaqua.2011.07.020.

Harter, S. (1990). Issues in the self-concept of children and adolescents. In A.M. La Greca (Ed.), *Through the eyes of the child: Obtaining self-reports from children and adolescents* (pp. 292-325). Boston, MA: Allyn and Bacon.

Harvey, J. B. (1996). *The Abilene paradox,* San Francisco, CA: Jossey-Bass.

Hecker, T. (2007). Workplace mobbing: a discussion for librarians, *Journal of Academic Leadership, 33*(44), 439-445. doi:10.1016/j. acalib2007.03003.

Herman, J. (1997). *Trauma and recovery: The aftermath of violence-from domestic abuse to political terror.* New York, NY: Basic Books.

Hindelang, M.S., Gottfredson, M., & Garofalo. J. (1978). *Victims of personal crime*. Cambridge, MA: Ballinger.

Hingson R.W., & Howland J. (2002). Comprehensive community interventions to promote health: Implications for college-age drinking problems. *Journal of Studies on Alcohol Supplement*, 14:226-240

Hinton, E. (2003). Microinequities: when small sights lead to hugh problems in the workplace. Retrieved from Diversity inc.com.www.magazine.org/content/files/microinequities.pdf .

Hoag, F. (2004). Implementation mechanisms for codes of conduct. *Study prepared for The World Book International Finance Corporation*. Retrieved from www. Gcgf.org/ifcept/economics… implementation&mechanisms.pdf.

Hochheiser, R. M. (1998*).* Workplace violence: A descriptive study of a major fortune 500 company [Abstract]. *Dissertation Abstracts International, 58*, 4725.

Hodson, R., Lopez, S., & Roscigno, V. (2006). Chaos and abuse of power: workplace bullying in organizational and international context*. Work and Occupation, 33*(4), 382-416. doi:10.1177/0730888406292885

Hoel, S. (2004 December 20). Bullying at work gains visibility. *Seattle Times,* p.1.

Hoel, S., & Cooper, C. (2000). *Destructive conflict and bullying at work.* Manchester/UK:University of Manchester.

Hoel, H., Rayner C., & Cooper, C.L. (1999).Workplace bullying. In C. L. Cooper & T. Robertson (Eds.). *Organizational Psychology, 14,* 195-229. New York, NY:John Wiley & Sons.

Hoel, H. & Salin, D. (2003). Organizational antecedents of workplace bullying. In S. Einarsen, H. Hoel, D. Zapf & C. Cooper (Eds.), *Bullying and educational abuse in the workplace: International perspectives in research and practice* (pp. 203-218).

Hoel, H., Einarsen, S., Cooper, C. (2003). Organizational effects of bullying. In S. Einarsen, H. Hoel, D. Zapf, C. Cooper (Eds.), *Bullying and emotional abuse in the workplace: International perspectives in research and practice* (pp. 145-161).

Hoepfl, M. C. (1997). Choosing qualitative research: A primer for technology education researchers. *Journal of Technology Education, 9*(1), 47-63.

Hogh, A. & Dofradottir, A. (2001). Coping with bullying in the workplace. *European Journal of Work and Organizational Psychology, 10*(4), 485-495. doi:10.1080/135943000825.

Hogh, A., Hansen, A., Mikkelsen, E. & Persson, R. (2011). Exposure to negative acts at work, psychological stress reaction and physiological stress responses. *Journal of Psychosomatic Research, 73*, 47-52. doi:10.1016/j.psycheces.

Hollander, E. P. (1958). Conformity, status and idiosyncrasy credit. *Psychological Review, 65,* 117-127. doi:10.1037/h00042501.

Hollander, E. P. (1961). Some effects of perceived status on responses to innovative behavior. *Journal of Abnormal- Social Psychology, 63,* 247-250. doi:10.1037/h0048240.

Hong, J.S.; Espelage, D.L.; Sterzing, P.R. (2015). Understanding the antecedents of adverse peer relationships among early adolescents in the United States: An ecological systems analysis. Youth and Society, 1-24. doi:10.1177/0044118X15569215

Horstein, H. A. (1996). *Brutal bosses and their prey*. New York, NY: Riverhead Books.

Hseih, F. & Shannon, S. (2005). Three approaches to qualitative research. *Quality Health Resources 15*(9), 1277-1288. doi:10.1177/104973230576687

Hudson, R., Roscigno, V. J., & Lopez, S. H. (2006). Chaos and abuse of power: Workplace bullying in organizational and interactional context, *Work and Occupations, 33,* 382-416. doi:10.1177/07308888/406292885.

Hutchinson, M., Vickers, H., Jackson, D. & Wilkes, L. (2010). Bullying as circuits of power. *Administrative Theory and Praxis, 32*(1), 25-47. doi:10.2753/ATP1084-1806320102

Janis, I. (1972). *Victims of group think.* Boston, MA: Houghton-Mifflin Company.

Janoff-Bulmann, R. (1992). Shattered assumptions: Toward a new psychology of trauma, New York, NY: Free Press.

Jenkins, M., Zapf, D., Winefield, H. & Sanis, A. (2012). Bullying allegations from the accused bully's perspective. *British Journal of Management, 23*(4), 489-501. doi:10.100.1111j.1467.8551.

Jennifer, D., Cowie H. & Ananiadou, K. (2003). Perceptions and experiences of workplace bullying in five different working populations, *Aggressive Behavior, 29*, 489-496. doi: 10.1002/ab.10055

Jowers, K. (2015, June). "Dependa" bashing: Mudslinging stun military spouses," Military Times Online, June 22, 2015, p. 7. Retrieved from http://www.militarytimes.com/story/military/2015/06/22/dependapotamus-bashing-spouses-strike-back/27522075/

Judge, T.A. & Bono, J.E. (2001) A rose by another name: Are self-esteem, generalized self-effacy, neuroticism, and losses of control indicators of a common construct? In B.W. Roberts & R. Hogan (Eds.,), *Personality psychology in the workplace (pp. 93-118).* Washington D.C. American Psychological Associates. doi:10.1037/10434-004.

Keashly, L. & Jagatic, K., (2000). The nature, extent, and impact of emotional abuse in the workplace: Results of a statewide survey. Paper presented at the Academy of Management Conference. Toronto.

Keashly, L. & Neuman, J.H. (2004). Bullying in the workplace: Its impact and management. *Employee Rights and Employment Policy Journal, 8*(2), 335-73. Retrieved from http://www.Lexis nexis.com.library.capella. edu.

Kelman, H.C. (1982). Ethical issues in different social science methods. *In T.L. Beauchamp; R.R. Faen, R.J. Wallace, Jr., and L. Walters (Eds.). Ethical Issues in Social Sciences Research* (pp. 40-98), Baltimore, MD & London, UK: The John Hopkins University Press.

Klein, A.S., Masi, R.J., & Weidner II, C.K. (1995). Organization culture, distribution and amount of control, and perceptions of quality: An empirical study of linkages. *Group Organization Management*, June, *20*, 122-148. doi: 10.1177/1059601195202004

Kruger, D. & Stones, C. R. (1981). An introduction to phenomenological psychology. Pittsburgh: Duquesne University Press. Retrieved from Project MUSE database. http://muse.jhu.edu/books/9780820706030

Kvale, S. (1996). *Interviews: An introduction to qualitative research interviewing*, Thousand Oaks, CA: Sage Publications.

La Montague, A. G., Kegel, T., Louicl, A. M., Ostgry, A. & Lansbergis, P. (2007). A systematic review of the job stress intervention evaluation literature, 1990- 2005. *International Journal of Occupational and Environmental Health, 13,* 268-280. doi:10.1179/.

Landry C. (1999). *The creative city: A toolkit for urban innovation.* London, England: Routledge.

Lawrence, J. & Tar, U. (2013). The use of grounded theory technique as a practical tool for qualitative data collection and analysis. *Electronic*

Journal of Business Research Methods, 11(1), 29-40. Retrieved from http://www.ejbrm.com.

Lazarus, R.S. & Folkman, S. (1984). *Stress, appraisal, and coping.* New York, NY: Springer.

Lee, C.H. (2011). An ecological systems approach to bullying behaviors among middle school students in the United States. *Journal of Interpersonal Violence, 26*(8), 1664-1693. doi:10.1177/0886260510370591

Lewis S.E. & Orford, J. (2005). Women's experiences in workplace bullying: Changes in social relationships. *Community and Applied Social Psychology, 15*, 29-47. doi:10.1002/casp.807.

Leymann, H. (1990). Mobbing and psychological terror at workplaces, *Violence and Victims, 5*(2), 119-26. Retrieved from http://www.mobbingportal. com/LeymannV%26V1990(3).pdf

Leymann, H. (1992). Leymann's inventory of psychological terror. Violen, Norway: Karlskronna.

Leymann, H. (1996). The content and development of mobbing at work. *European Journal of Work and Organizational Psychology, 5*(2), 165-184. doi: 10.1080/13594329608414853

Leymann, H. & Gutavson, A. (1996). Mobbing at work and the development of post- traumatic stress disorder, *European Journal of Work and Organizational Psychology, 5*(2). doi:10.1080/135943296084148.8.

Liden, R. C., Sparrow, R. T., & Wayne, S. J. (1997). Leader-member exchange theory: The past and potential for the future. In G.R. Ferris (Ed). *Research in personnel and human resource management* (vol. 15, pp, 47-120). Greenwich, CT: JAI Press.

Liefooghe, A. & MacKenzie-Davey, K. (2001). Accounts of workplace bullying: The Role of the organization. *European Journal of Work and Educational Psychology, 10*(4), *375-392.* doi:10.1080/13594320143000762.

Likert, R. (1967). *The Human Organization: Its Management and Value*, New York, NY: Harper & Row.

Longzeng, W., Liqun, W., & Chun, H. (2011). Dispositional antecedents and consequences of workplace ostracism: An empirical examination. *Front. Bus.Res China 5,* 23-44. doi:10.1007/571782-011-0119-2.

Lorenz, K. (1996). *On aggression.* Munich: Deutscher Taschenbach Verlog Gmt H. & Co.KG.

Lutgen-Sandvik, P. & Davenport-Sypher, B. (Eds.) (2009). *Destructive organizational communication: Processes, consequences, and constructive ways of organizing.* New York, NY: Routledge.

Malloy, D.P. (1998). Workplace violence: A descriptive study of a major fortune 500 company. *Dissertation Abstracts International, 58,* 4725.

Marshall, C. & Rossman, G. (1989). *Designing qualitative research.* Thousand Oaks, CA: Sage Publications.

Matthiesen, S. B. (2006). *Bullying at work: Antecedents and outcomes.* [Doctoral Thesis]. Retrieved from http://hdl.handle.net/1956/1550/ doi:13594320143000753.

Matthiesen, S. B. & Einarsen, S. (2004). Psychiatric distress and symptoms of PTSD among victims of bullying at work. *British Journal of Guidance and Counselling, 32*(3), 335-356. doi:10.1080/030698804100017235 58.

Matusewitch, E. (1996). Constructive discharge: When a resignation is really a termination. *Employment Discrimination Report, 6,* 1-5.

Maughan, J. (2010). What is the legal definition of harassment? Life 123. Retrieved from www. http://posts. Fansox.com/5p6v3

McLaughlin, K. (2014). Workplace bullying: A silent epidemic. SHRM Society for Human Resource Management (online). Retrieved from http://

www.shrm.org/publications/hrmagazine/editorialcontent/2014/1014/ pages/1014-viewpoint-workplace-bullying.aspx.

Mellington, T. (2004, November 11). Bullies force employees out of jobs. *AGB Bullying News*, pp 3. Retrieved from www.webspawner.news/national. com/users/news 3/index.html.

Mikkelsen, B. (1995). *Methods for development work and research.* Thousand Oaks, CA: Sage.

Mikkelson, E., Einarsen, S., & Cooper, H. (2002). Basic assumptions and symptoms of post-traumatic stress among victims of bullying at work. *European Journal of work and organizational Psychology,* 11, 87-111. doi:10.1080/1359432 0143000861.

Mikkelson, E. & Einarsen, S. (2002). Relationships between exposure to bullying at work and psychological and psychosomatic health complaints: The role of state negative affectivity and, general self-efficacy .*Scandinavian Journal of Psychology, 43(5)*, 397-405. doi:10.1111/1467-9450.00307/ pdf.

Miner, J. B. (1992). *Industrial organizational psychology,* New York, NY: McGraw-Hill.

Mir, J. A. (2009). *Organizational transformation*, published by Key Organizational Processes. Retrieved from http://asifjmir.wordpress. com/2009/05/18 key organizational-processes/trackback/.

Mitchell, A. (2010). *Complex PTSD: Devastating health effects from workplace bullying.* www.workplace bullying, org/2011/09/30/suite 101/#more-6212.

Moir, S., Thomson, M. & Kelleher, C. (2011). *Unfinished business: Building equality for women in the construction trades.* University of Massachusetts Boston: Labor Resources Center Publications.

Retrieved from http://scholarworks.umb.edu/cgi/ viewcontent. cgi?article=1004&context=lrc_pubs.

Morrison, R (2008). Negative relationships in the workplace: Associations with organizational commitment, cohesion, job satisfaction and intention to turnover. *Journal of Management and Organization, 14*(4), 330-344. doi:10.5172/jmo.837.14.4.330

Myers, M. D. (1997). Qualitative research in information systems. *Management Information Systems Quarterly, 21*(2), 221-242. Retrieved from https://www.researchgate.net/profile/Michael_Myers4/publication/220260372_Qualitative_Research_in_Information_Systems/links/00b7d51803a28485c3000000.pdf

Namie, G. & Namie, R., (2000). *The bully at work: What you can do to stop the hurt and reclaim your dignity on the job.* Naperville, Ill: Source Books, Inc.

Namie, G. (2003). Workplace bullying: Escalated incivility, *Ivey Business Journal, 68,* 1-6. Retrieved from http://www.workplacebullying.org/multi/pdf/N-N-2003A.pdf

Needham, A. (2004). *Workplace bullying: A costly business secret.* London, UK: Penguin.

Nielsen, M. B. & Einarsen, S. (2012). Outcomes of workplace bullying: A meta-analytic review. *Work and Stress, 26*(4), 309-332. doi:10.1080/02678373. 2012.734709.

Nils, M., Lau, B., Ruse, T., & Moen, B. (2009). Association of psychosocial factors and bullying at individual and department levels among naval and military personnel. *Journal of Psychosomatic Research*, 66(4), 343-351. doi:10.1016/j.jpsychores.

Olsen, H. (2008). *Mediation is not the answer to bullying.* Workplaces Against Violence in Employment (WAVE online). Retrieved from http://www.wave.org.nz/index.php/mediation.

O'Leary-Kelly, A.M., Duffy, M.K., & Griffin, R.W. (2000). Construct confusion in the study of antisocial behavior at work. *Research in Personnel and Human Resources Management, 18,* 275-304. Retrieved from https://www.econbiz.de/Record/construct-confusion-in-the-study-of-antisocial-work-behavior-leary-kelly-anne/10006904182.

Olweus, D. (1991). Bully/victim problems among schoolchildren: Basic facts and effects of a school-based intervention program. In D. Pepler & K. Rubin (Eds.), *The development and treatment of childhood aggression* (pp. 411-448). Hillsdale, NJ: Erlbaum.

Olweus, D. (1993). *Bullying at school: What we know and what we can do.* Cambridge, MA: Blackwell.

O'Moore, M., Sergue, M., McGuire, L., Smith, M., & Seigne, E. (1998). Victims of bullying at work in Ireland, *Journal of Occupational Health & Safety, Australia & N. Zealand, 14*(6), 56-74. doi:10.1080/0303391 0.1998.10558195.

Paine, L.S. (1994). Managing organizational integrity. *Harvard Business Review, 72*(2), 106-117. Retrieved from http://actoolkit.unprme.org/wp-content/resourcepdf/201106171723110.Managing%20organizational%20integrity.pdf

Patton, M. D. (1980). *Qualitative research and evaluation methods.* Thousand Oaks, CA: Sage Publications.

Perkins, H.W., & Berkowitz, A.D. (1986). Perceiving the community norms of alcohol use among students: Some research implications for campus alcohol education programming. *International Journal of the Addictions,* 21, 961–976.

Peterson, C., Maier, S., & Seligman, M. (1995). *Learned helplessness: A theory for the age of personal control.* New York, NY: Oxford University Press.

Petri, H. (1998). *The road to ruin.* Paper presented at the Bullying at Work Conference, Staffordshire University, Staffordshire, UK.

Peyton, P.R. (2003). *Dignity at work, eliminate bullying and create a positive working environment.* London, UK: Taylor, & Francis Group.

Pratto, F., Sidanius, J., & Levin, S. (2006). Social dominance theory and the dynamics of intergroup relations: Taking stock and looking forward. *European Review of Social Psychology, 17,* 271-320. Retrieved from http://isites.harvard.edu/fs/docs/icb.topic895260.files/PrattoSidaniusLevin_2006.pdf

Punch, M. (1986). *The politics and ethics of fieldwork.* Newbury Park, CA: Sage.

Punch, M. (1994). *Politics and ethics in qualitative research*: London, UK: Sage.

Quince, L. (1999). Workplace bullying in NHS community trust: staff questionnaire survey. *British Medical Journal, 318,* 228-232. doi:10.1136/bmj.318.7178.228.

Ramsey, R.D. (2002). Conflict escalation and coping with workplace bullying. *European Journal of Work and Organizational Psychology, 10*(14), 1464. doi:10.1080/1359432014000834.

Randall, P. (1997). *Adult bullying, perpetrators and victims.* London: Routledge.

Randle, J. (2003). Bullying in the nursing profession. *Journal of Advanced Nursing. 43(4),* 395-401. doi:10.1046/j.1365-2648.2005.02728.

Rathery, G. (2005). *Bashing the bully pulpit.* VA: American Society for Training and Development.

Rayner, M. (1999*)*. Workplace bullying: Do something, *Journal of Occupational Health & Safety, Australia and New Zealand, 14*(6)*, 581-5.

Rayner, C., Hoel, H., & Cooper, G.L. (2002). *Workplace bullying: What we know, who is to blame, and what can we do*? London, UK: Taylor & Francis.

Rayner, C. & Keashly, L (2004). Bullying at work: A perspective from Britain and North America. In E. Fox, S. Fox & P. Spector (Eds.), *Counterproductive work behavior: Investigations of actors and targets.* Washington D.C: APA Press. http://dx.doi.org/10.1037/10893-011

Rhodes, S. (1978) Major influences on employee attendance: a process model, *Journal of Applied Psychology, 63*, 391-407. 10.2753/ATP1084-1806320105.

Rhodes, C., Pullen, A., Vickers, M., Clegy, S., & Pitsis, A. (2010). Violence and Workplace bullying: What are an organizations ethical responsibilities: *Administrative Theory and Praxis, 32* (1), 96-115.

Richardson, J.E. & McCord, L.B. (2001). Are workplace bullies sabotaging your ability to compete? *Graziadio Business Review, 4*(4). Retrieved from https://gbr.pepperdine.edu/2010/08/are-workplace-bullies-sabotaging-your-ability-to-compete/

Robinson, S.L. & O'Leary-Kelly, A. (1998). Monkey see, monkey do: The influence of work groups on the antisocial behavior of employees. *Academy of Management Journal, 41,* 658-672. doi:10.2307/256963.

Rosenberg, M. (1965). *Society and the adolescent self-image*, Princeton, NJ: Princeton University Press. doi:10.1126/science.148.3671.804.

Rowe, M. (1990). The minutiae of discrimination: The need for support. In Forisha, B. & Goldman, B. Barriers to equality: The power of subtle discrimination, *The Employee Responsibilities and Rights Journal, 3*(2), 153-163.

Sampson, R.J., & Lauritsen, J.L. (1994). *Violent victimization and offending: Individual-, situational-, and community level risk factors*. In Understanding and Preventing Violence, vol. 3, edited by A.J. Reiss and J.A. Roth. Washington, DC: National Academy Press, pp. 1–114.

Salin, D. (2003). Ways of explaining workplace bullying: A review of enabling, motivating and precipitating structures and processes in the work environment. *Human Relations, 56*(10), 1213-1232. doi:10.1177/0987267035610003.

Salin, D. (2005). Workplace bullying among business professionals: Prevalence, gender differences and the role of organizational politics. *Swedish School of Economics and Business Administration, 7*(3). Retrieved from www.pistes.revued.org/3159.

Saunders, D. G. (1994). Post-traumatic stress symptom profiles of battered women: A comparison of survivors in two settings, *Violence and Victims, 9*(1), 31-44. Retrieved from http://www.proquest.com.library. capella.edu.

Schat, A. & Frone, M. (2011). Exposure to psychological aggression at work and job Performance: The mediating role of job attitudes and personal health. *Work and Stress, 25*(1), 23-40. doi:10.1080/02678373.2011.56 3133

Schmidt, K., Neubach, R. & Heuer, H. (2007). Self- control demands, cognitive control Deficits, and burnout. *Work and Stress, 21,* 142-154. doi:1080/02678370201431680.

Schneider, B. (1975). *Organizational climates*: An essay. *Personnel Psychology, 40,* 437-454. doi:10.1111/j.1744-6570.1975.tb01386.x

Scott, M. & Strandling, S., (1994). Post traumatic stress disorder without the trauma. *British Journal of Clinical Psychology. 33,* 71-74. doi:10.1111/j.2044-8260.1994.tb01095.x

Seago, J.A. (1996). Work group culture, stress and hostility: correlations with organizational outcomes. *The Journal of Nursing Administration.* 2(6), 39-47.

Sepler, F. (2010). Workplace bullying: What it is and what you do about it. Retrieved from http://seplerblog.files.wordpress.com/2012/05/cle-handout-2010.pdf.

Shanghassy, J., Zechmeister, J. & Zechmeister, E. (2000). *Essentials of research methods in psychology* (1ˢᵗ edition). New York City, NY: McGraw-Hill.

Shehan, M. (1999). Workplace bullying: Responding with some emotional intelligence. *International Journal of Manpower. 20*(1/2) pp. 57.

Sidanius, J., & Pratto, F. (1999). Social dominance: An intergroup theory of social hierarchy and oppression. New York: Cambridge University Press.

Siemer, M., Marcus, I., & Gross, J. (2007). Same situation-different emotion: How appraisals shape our emotions. *Emotions, 7*(3), 592-600. doi:10.1037/1528-3542733592.

Simon, N. (2010, November 14). Stress on the job raises the risk of heart disease in women. *AARP Bulletin.* Retrieved from www.aarp.org/health.../job strain_raises_risk_of-heart_disease.html.

Sinclair, J., Ironside, M., and Seifect, R. (1996). Classroom struggle, market oriented education reforms and their impact on the teacher labour process. *Work, Employment and Society, 10,* 641-661. doi:10.1177/0900517096104002.

Skogstad, T., Matthiesen, A., & Einarsen, S. (2007). Organizational changes: A precursor of bullying at work? *International Journal of Organization Theory and Behavior, 10,* 58-94. Retrieved from http://folk.uib.no/pspsm/documents/Org-change-Skogstad-Matthiesen-Einarsen.pdf

Smart, R. & Leary, M. R. (2009). Reactions to discrimination, stigmatization, ostracism, and other forms of interpersonal rejection: A multimotive model. *Psychological Review, 116*(2*): 365-83. doi:10.1037/90015250.

Solorzano, D., Ceja, M., & Yosso, T. (2000). Critical race theory, racial microaggressions, and campus racial climate: The experiences of African American college students. *Journal of Negro Education, 69*(1/2), 60. Retrieved from https://www.middlesex.mass.edu/RLOs/748/Critical-Race-Theory.pdf

Spratlen, L. (1995). Interpersonal conflict which includes mistreatment in a university workplace. *Violence and Victims, 10*(4), 285-297.

Strauss, A.L., & Corbin, J.M. (1998). *Basics of qualitative research.* London: Sage.

Sue, D. (2010). Microaggressions: More than just race: Can microaggressions be directed at women or gay people? *Psychology Today,* Retrieved from https://www.psychologytoday.com/blog/microaggressions-in-everyday-life/201011/microaggressions-more-just-race.

Sue, D.W., Capodilupo, C.M., Tonno, G.C., Bucceni, J.M., Holder, A.M.B., Nadal, K.L., & Esquilin, M. (2007). Racial microaggressions in everyday life. *American Psychologist, 62,* 271-286. http://dx.doi.org/10.1037/0003-066X.62.4.271

Taylor, C. (1976). Hermaneutics and politics. In Critical Sociology: Selected Readings, Connerton, P (ed.), p. 153-193. Penguin Books: Harmondsworth.

Tepper, B. (2000). Consequences of abusive supervision, *Academy of Management Journal, 43*(2)*,* 178-190. doi:10.2307/1556375

Tepper, B., Uhl-Bien, M., Kohut, G., Rogelberg, S., Lockhart, D., and Ensley, M. (2006). Subordinates' resistance and managers' evaluations of subordinates. *Journal of Management, 32,* 185-209. doi:10.1177/0149206305280102.

Tracy, S. J., (2010). Compassion: Cure for an ailing workplace. *Communication Currents, 5(6).* Retrieved from http://www.nat com.org/comm currents Article.aspx?id=2147483917.

Tracy, S.J., Lutgen-Sandvik, P., & Alberts, J.K. (2006). Nightmares, demons and slaves: Exploring the painful metaphors of workplace bullying. *Management Communication Quarterly, 20*(2), 148-185. doi:10.1177/0893318906.

Trochim, W.M., Marcus, S.E., Weld, P.C., Masse, L.C & Richard, R.P. (2008). The evaluation of large research initiatives. *American Journal of Evaluation, 29*(1). doi:10.1177/1098214007309280.

UNISON (1997). *UNIS member's experience of bullying at work*: London, UK: UNISON. Update Medical University (2010). *stress Reduction/ mindful eating.* Retrieved from http://www.upstate.edu/stress/work. php.suny update-syracuse medical university-ny.

Ursin, H. & Eriksen, H.R. 92004). The cognitive activation theory of stress. *Psychoneuroendocrinology 29*(5), 567-92. doi:10.1016/50306-4630 (03) 00091-X. PMID 15015041082.

Van de Vliet (1998). Conflict and conflict management. In Drouth, P.D., Thierry, H. and de Wolf, J. (Eds.), Handbook of Work and Organizational Psychology. *Personnel Psychology.* East Suxxex: Psychology Press Ltd.

van Dam, A., Keijsers, G.P.J., Eling, P.A.T.M. & Becker, E.S. (2012*).* Impaired cognitive performance and responsiveness to reward in burnout patients: Two years later. *Work and Stress, 26*(4). doi:10.1080/02678 373.2012.737550.

van der Kolk, B., Roth, S., Pelcovitz, D., Sunday, S., & Spinazzola, J. (2005). Disorders of extreme stress: The empirical foundation of a complex adaptation to trauma. *Journal of Traumatic Stress,* 18, 389-399. Retrieved from http://www.traumacenter.org/products/pdf_files/ specialissuecomplextraumaoct2006jts3.pdf

Van Sell, M., Brief, A.P. and Schuler, R.S. (1981). Role conflict and role ambiguity: integration of the literature and directions for future research. *Human Relations, 34*, 43-71. doi:10.1177/01872678103400104.

Vanderstaay, S.L. (2005). Learning from longitudinal research in criminology and the health sciences. *Reading Research Quarterly, July/August 2006. 413*, 328-350. doi:101598/rrq41322.

Vartia-Vaananen, M. (2002). Workplace bullying: A study on the work environment, well-being and health (doctoral dissertation). Dept. of Psychology, University of Helsinki. Retrieved from http://ethesis. helsinki.fi/julkaisut/hum/psyko/vk/vartia-vaananen/workplac.pdf

Vergun, D. (2012). Zero tolerance in army for bullying and hazing. Retrieved from https: www.army.mil-the-official homepage of the United States Army.

Vickers, M. H. (2006). Towards employee wellness: Rethinking bullying paradoxes and masks, *Employee Responsibilitiesand Rights Journal,* 18, 267-281. doi:10.1007/s/0672-006-9023x.

Vinokur, A.D., Price, R. & Caplan, R. (1996). Hard times and hurtful partners: How financial strain affects depression and relationship satisfaction of unemployed persons and their spouses. *Journal of Personality and Social Psychology, 71,* 166-179. Retrieved from http://www. hbftpartnership.com/documents/uploadResources/Price_1996-finstraindepressionunemployment.pdf

Vinokur, A.D. & Van Ryan, M. (1993). Social support and undermining in close relationships: Their independent effect on mental health in unemployed persons *Journal of Personality and Social Psychology, 65,* 350-359. http://dx.doi.org/10.1037/0022-3514.65.2.350

Voss, M. Fiderus, B. and Diderichsen, F. (2001). Physical, psychosocial and organizational factors: a study based on sweden post, *Journal of Occupational and Environmental Medicine*, *58*, 178-184. doi:10.1136/ oem.58.3.175.

Wegner, D. M. & Smart, L. (1997). Deep cognitive activation: A new approach to the unconscious. *Journal of Counseling and Clinical Psychology, 65*(6), 984-995. http://dx.doi.org/10.1037/0022-006X.65.6.984

Weiss, H.M. & Cropanzao R. (1996). Affective events theory: A theoretical discussion of the structure, causes, and consequences of affective experiences at work. *Research in Organizational Behavior*, 18, 1-74. Retrieved from https://www.msu.edu/course/psy/962/Weiss%20&%20 Cropanzano%20(1996)%20-%20AET.pdf.

Welman, J. C., & Kruger, S.J. (1999). *Research methodology for the business and administrative sciences.* Capetown, South Africa: Oxford University Press.

Westhaus, K. (1998*). Eliminating professors: A guide to the dismissal process.* Leviston, N.Y: Kemper Collegium Publication, The Edwin Mellen Press.

White, S. (2004). A psychodynamic perspective of workplace bullying: Containment, boundaries and futile search for recognition. *British Journal of Guidance and Counseling, 32*(3), 269-280. doi:10.1080/03 069881410091723512.

William, K. D. (2007). Ostracism. *Annual Review of Psychology: 58,* 425-452. doi:10.1146/annurev.psych.58.110405.085641.

William, K. D. & Sommer, K. L. (1997). Social ostracism by co- workers: Does rejection lead to loafing or compensation? *Personality and Social Psychology Bulletin, 23*, 693-706. doi:10.117710146167287237003.

Willness, C.R., Steel, P. & Lee, K. (2007). A meta-analysis of the antecedents and consequences of workplace sexual harassment, *Personnel Psychology, 60*, 127-162. doi:10.1111/j.1744-6570200700067x.

Wilson, J. P. (1980). Conflict, stress and growth: The effects of the Vietnam war on psychosocial development among Vietnam veterans. In C. K. Figley and S. Laventman (Eds.). *Strangers at home: Vietnam veterans since the war.* Santa Barbara, CA: Praeger Press.

Wilson, C.B. (1991). U.S. businesses suffer from workplace trauma, *Personnel Journal, 70*, 47.

Winter, G. (2000). A comparative discussion of the notion of 'validity' and 'reliability' in qualitative and quantitative research. *The Qualitative Report, 4*(3), 1-14. Retrieved from http://nsuworks.nova.edu/tqr/vol4/iss3/4

Wong, G., Derthick, E., David, E.J.R., Saw, A., & Okazaki, S. (2014). The *what*, the *why* and the *how*: A review of racial microaggressions research in psychology. *Race and Society, 6,* 181-2005. doi:10.1007/s12552-013-9107-9.

Workplace Bullying Institute Website (2014). Retrieved from http:www. Workplace institute.org.

Wyatt, J., & Hare, C. (1997). *Work abuse: How to recognize it and survive it.* Rochester, VT: Schenkman Books.

Yamada, D. (2000). The phenomenon of workplace bullying and the need for status-blind hostile work environment protection. *Georgetown Law Journal, 88*, 475. http://ssrn.com/abstract=1303690

Yamada, D. (2003). Workplace bullying and the law: towards a transnational consensus? In Stale Einarsen, et al., (Eds.). *Bullying and Emotional Abuse in the Workplace: International Perspectives In Research and Practice*, London, UK: Taylor & Francis.

Yamada, D. (2004). The role of the law in combating workplace mobbing and bullying, in Kenneth Westhus (Ed.), *Workplace Mobbing in Academe: Reports from Twenty Universities.* Lewiston, New York, NY: Mellen Press.

Yamada, D. (2015). *Multiple disciplinary responses to workplace bullying: Systems, synergy and sweat.* Paper presented at the Sixth International Conference on Workplace Bullying. Montreal, Canada. Retrieved from http://www.workplacebullying.org/ research/conferences/images/ dymontreal.pdf.

Zapf, D. & Einarsen, S. (2003). *Individual antecedents of bullying: victims and perpetrators: Bullying And emotional abuse in the workplace: International perspectives in research and practice.* London, England: Taylor & Francis.

Zapf, D. & Gross, C. (2001). Conflict escalation and coping with workplace bullying: A replication and extension, *European Journal of Work and Organizational Psychology, 10*, 497-522. doi:10.10891359432013000834.

Zapf, D., Knory, C., & Kulla, M. (1996). On the relationship between mobbing factors, and job content, social work environment, and health outcomes. *European Journal of Work and Occupational Psychology, 5*(2), 215-237. doi:10.1080/13594329608414856.

Zellars, K. L., Tepper, B. T. & Duffy, M. K. (2002). Abusive supervision and Subordinate's organizational citizenship behavior. *Journal of Applied Psychology, 87,* 1068-1076. doi:10.1037/0021.9010.934721

Appendix A:

Informed Consent Form

Linda Mata, doctoral learner under the direction of Dr. Alphonso Bellalmy in the School of Business at Capella University, is conducting a research study, entitled *Workplace Bullying: A Phenomological Study of Its Effects on Targets and Organizational Productivity*, to explore causes of workplace bullying and provide information that may add to future research and may lead to ending bullying in the workplace and also to provide information that may be helpful to victims of bullying. You are invited to participate in this research by relating incidents of bullying you have experienced with a face-to-face or telephone interview. You have been invited to participate because you expressed an interest in giving your responses to the questions to be presented concerning workplace bullying that you have either experienced or witnessed as a bystander. No risks to you are anticipated in the study.

The possible benefits of your participation in the research are you may provide information that may lead to a better understanding of the affects of the bullying phenomena and add to future research that may end bullying in the workplace.

The researcher will contact you if the researcher learns of new information that could change your decision about participating in this study.

The results of this study will be published, but your name or identity will not be revealed.

In order to maintain confidentiality of your records, the researcher will not reveal your identity and safeguard your information and responses.

If you choose not to participate or choose to withdraw from the study, you may do so at any time, there will be no penalty.

You will be charged no costs to participate and will not be paid to participate.

If you have any questions about your rights, suffer any harm because you participated in this research project, have any concerns about the research process, or would like to discuss anyunanticipated problems related to this research, please contact The Capella Human Research and Protections Office at 1-888-227-3552, extension 4716. Your identity and concerns will be kept confidential.

By signing this form, you are saying (1) that you have read this form or have had it read to you and (2)that you understand this form, the research study, and its risks and benefits. The researcher will be happy to answer any questions you have about the research. If you have any questions, please feel free to contact Linda Mata at (360)459-1299 or LM3131@capella.edu.

If at any time you feel pressured to participate of if you have any questions about your rights or this form, please call the Chair of the Institutional Review Board through the Research & Scholarship Office at (612)977-5385.

Note: By signing below, you are telling the researchers "Yes," you participate in this study. Please keep one copy of this form for your records.

Your Name (please print):_____

Your Signature: _____

Date: _____

I certify that this form includes all information concerning the study relevant to the protection of the rights of the participants, including the nature and purpose of this research, benefits, risks, costs, and any experimental procedures.

I have described the rights and protections afforded to human research participants and have done nothing to pressure, coerce, or falsely entice this person to participate. I am available to answer the participant's questions and have encouraged him or her to ask additional questions at any time during the course of the study.

Investigator's Signature: _____
Investigator's Name: Linda Mata.

Appendix B.

Demographic Questionnaire

First Name _____ MI _____ Last Name _____

Mailing Address _____

Office Phone Number _____ E-mail Address _____

Male: _____ Female: _____

What is your age? Under 27: _____ 28-55: _____ 56-73: _____ Over 73: _____

Ethnic Background of participant (Optional)

Black: _____ Asian: _____ Hispanic: _____ Caucasian: _____ Other: _____

Participant's country of origin: _____

Current Employment Status: _____

Military Status: _____

    Active Military: _____

    Retired Military: _____

Educational Level:

    High School Graduate: _____

    College Graduate or Semester Hours: _____

    Professional Experience: _____

Appendix C.

Design of Interview Questions

These questions will be asked in a semi-structured environment to allow the participants to freely answer open-ended questions and ask additional questions. The objective of the interview is to encourage the participant's to continue revealing their personal experiences with workplace bullying and describe how they have been affected by bullying. Nine questions have been designed that will gather critical information about the effects of bullying. These questions will be presented to the participants. They are:

1. Do you feel you have experienced or witnessed workplace bullying?
2. Did this experience affect your physical health?
3. Did this experience affect your psychological health?
4. Did this experience affect your self-esteem?
5. Did this experience affect your job satisfaction?
6. Did your experience affect your perspective about your organization?
7. Did bullying cause you to change your career?
8. Did this experience affect your relationship with co-workers, family members, friends, and others both within and outside your work environment?
9. Do you think you organization's culture contributed to your experience? If so, why?

More probing questions will be drawn from other instruments and studies such as Leymann's Inventory of Psychological Terror (1990a), Studies by Salin (2003), Rosenberg's Self-Esteem Scale (1965), studies of Mellington

(2004), Morrison (2008), Beasley et al., (1997), Petri (1998),Adams (1992), and Hodson, Lopez, & Roscigno (2006).

Leymann's Inventory of Psychological Terror is a 45-item questionnaire that was developed to establish the frequency of mobbing in an organization. The questions help to identify whether or not a victim of mobbing has suffered a breakdown of his/her "coping resources." This breakdown leads to feelings of desperation, total helplessness, a feeling of great rage about lack of legal remedies, and great anxiety and despair (Leymann, 1990).

Salin's (2003) study identifies negative behaviors that encompass bullying such as social isolation, rumors spread about victims, attacks on a victim's private life, and excessive criticism or monitoring of a victim's work. The Rosenberg Self-Esteem Scale is a 10-item Likert Scale with items answered on a 4 point scale from strongly agree to strongly disagree. The scale can be used to assess global self-esteem. Items on the scale statements: "At times do you think you are no good at all?" "On the whole, I am satisfied with myself," and "All in all, I am inclined to feel that I am a failure," (Rosenberg, 1965).

Studies of Mellington are found in The Australian Master OHS and Environment Guide 2nd Edition. Studies from this book demonstrate how an employee's feelings of insecurity may be linked to their prolonged having prolonged stress and failing physical and mental health (Mellington, 2007).

Morrison's study investigates the link between perceptions of negative workplace

relationships and organizational outcomes. The results of the study indicated that those with at least one negative relationship at work were significantly less satisfied with their job. They also reported less organizational commitment, were part of less cohesive workgroups and were likely to be planning to leave their job (Morrison, 2008).

Questions for this study derived from the studies of (Beasley et al., 1997), Petri (1998), and Adams (1992) focus on areas of their studies that identify conflicts in organizations that express themselves in aggression, whether between superior and subordinate or between colleagues and others in and outside of the workplace (Luzio-Lockett, 1995). This aggression escalates as persistent attacks are made on a person's personal and professional performance and may develop into a campaign of vindictiveness (Beasley & Rayner, 1997).

Questions for this study from works of Hodson, Lopez, & Roscigno (2006) relate to the roles of relational power and organizational chaos and the emergence of workplace bullying (Hodson et al., 2006). Their study suggests the need for organizations to eliminate the chaos in their organizations that create openings for abuse of power (Hodson et al., 2006).

The information used in these instruments and studies are linked to the concepts and research discussed in this study's literature review. Question number one helps to clarify if one's experiences can be defined as bullying and if they can be aligned with the process of bullying as identified in Chapter Two.

Questions 2-8, tests concepts of the affects of bullying on one's physical health, psychological **health, self-esteem, job satisfaction, perspective of organization and interpersonal relations. Question** 9, asks how a victim or bystander may feel the organization's culture contributed to bullying.

Each of these questions is discussed with concepts in the literature review of Chapter Two.

A gap exists in the literature because many questions are unanswered about the type of support needed to facilitate recognition of workplace bullying as targets struggle to identify and cope with bullying (Lewis, 2010). I will choose to use the questions formed in this study because they may help to further identify how bullying unfolds in the workplace and the degree in which it affects an individual's health and welfare.

APPENDIX D:

FIELD STUDY USING INTERVIEW QUESTIONS

A field study was conducted with 2 participants who volunteered to participate in the study and indicated they have experienced and/or witnessed bullying in the workplace. Both participants are middle-aged adults who have been employed for a government agency for over 10 years. The first participant, who I will identify as Participant A, is a female employee. The interview was conducted by telephone and lasted 35 minutes.

The second participant will be identified as Participant B. He is a male employee who said he has both experienced and witnessed bullying in his workplace. A face-to-face interview was conducted. The interview lasted 22 minutes. I explained confidentiality and privacy rules to both participants prior to the interview and assured them that they were under to obligation or pressure to answer any questions. Below are the questionnaire and their responses.

Interview Questions:

1. Do you feel you have experienced or witnessed bullying in the workplace?
    Participant A-yes;
    Participant B-yes.

Question to Probe: Derived from Leymann's Inventory of Psychological Terror (1990a); Questions c-f are derived from a study by Salin (2003).

A. How long were you a victim of or did you witness bullying?

Participant A-1 year;
Participant B-5 years.

B. Provide an example of a lie or lies that have been told about you to others?
Participant A-don't know;
Participant B-don't know.

C. Why do you feel you may have you been a victim of isolation?
Participant A-silent treatment from co-workers and won't respond to questions;
Participant B-no support from supervisor or credit given for good suggestions.

D. What statements were made to attack your attitude or your personal life?
Participant A- supervisor tries to make me feel life a failure and said "I bet your husband does everything at home and you don't do anything."
Participant B: none

E. Give an example or examples of instances when necessary information needed for your work was withheld from you.
Participant A-Was criticized for not knowing what parking lot was closed down when wasn't told.
Participant B-Never briefed on information

Needed and then criticized for not
Participant A-no;
Participant B-no

Impact of Bullying on Physical Health:

Questions to probe responses were derived from (Mellington 2004)
A. Did the bullying experience affect your Physical Health?
Participant A-don't know;
Participant B-maybe arthiritis pain in shoulders.

B. Have you suffered any stress-related illnesses? Such as heart disease or hypertension?

C. Have you suffered from any skin reactions, stress, headaches, diabetes mellitus, hair loss, or less immunity to colds and flus?

     Participant A-don't know;

     Participant B-don't know

Impact on Psychological Health:

Questions to probe responses were derived from (Mellington 2004)

A. Did the experience affect your psychological health?

     Participant A-feels stressed;

     Participant B

     Participant A-No;

     Participant B-No

C. Do you suffer from stress/irritability?

     Participant A-No;

     Participant B-Yes

D. Have you engaged in any self- behavior or abuse as alcoholism?

     Participant A-smoke cigarettes;

     Participant B-No

E. Have you noticed any panic attacks or Anxiety?

     Participant A-yes;

     Participant B-No

Impact on Self-Esteem:

Questions to probe responses taken from Rosenberg's Esteem Scale (1965)

A. Was your self-esteem affected by bullying?

     Participant A-Yes;

     Participant B-No, I won't let it happen

B. How much do you feel satisfied with yourself?

Participant A-feel satisfied;
Participant B-feel satisfied

C. At times do you feel useless? Why?
Participant A-No;
Participant B-No

D. Do you feel all in all, that you are inclined to fail, if so, why?
Participant A-No;
Participant B-No

Impact on Job Satisfaction:

A. Did bullying affect job satisfaction:
Participant A-No;
Participant B-Yes-unhappy about the way they do things.

Impact on Organizational Commitment:
Questions to Probe Response taken from Research of
Morrison(2008).

A. Did the experience affect your perception of your job?
Participant A-No;
Participant B-Yes- organziation is embedded with old ways and fears change

B. Do you feel less committed to your organization?
Participant A-No;
Participant B-Yes

C. Can you provide examples of negative experiences you have had with co-workers and supervisor
Participant A-Supervisor seemed to imply I was lazy when I am not;
Participant B-Supervisor is critical and does not give me credit for suggestions and then when she sees I had a good idea, she credits someone else.

Impact on Career:
Questions Used to Probe Reponses taken from Morrison (2008)

A. Did bullying cause you to change your career?

      Participant A-No;

      Participant B-No.

B. How has your experience impacted your ability to find another job/ choose a career?

      Participant A-don't know;

      Participant B-don't know

Impact on Family Members/Interpersonal Relationships:
Questions to Probe Responses derived from studies of
(Beasley et al., 1997; Petri, 1998; Adams, 1992).

A. Did this experience effect your relationships with co-workers, family members and Friends?

      Participant A-Yes;

      Participant B-No

B. What problems have you had or do you currently have with family members?

      Participant A-want to talk about it too much with husband and sometimes he doesn't want to hear about it so much.

C. Do often do you find yourself being more cynical, critical,and sarcastic and feel this be related to bullying/may be related to bullying?

      Participant A-a little cynical;

      Participant B-It makes you suspicious. A co- worker was bullied off his job and no one gave him support.

Bullying and Organizational Culture:
Questions to Probe Responses taken study by Hodson, Lopez and Roscigno (2006).

Do do you think the organization contributed to your bullying experiences? If so, how?

Participant A-don't know;

Participant B-Yes, Management has bullying embedded in the culture.

Discussion of Responses

The purpose of the study was to identify the reasons why the participants believed they have been bullied based upon the definition of bullying given to them and the negative acts researchers have identified that encompass bullying or may lead to bullying. Participant A was bullied for one year and Participant B for 5 years so in both cases the bullying has occurred for more than 6 months. Neither participant knew of any lies or rumors that has been circulated about them, But Participant A experienced social isolation and the "silent treatment" while Participant B felt a lack of support from the supervisor and received no credit for suggestions. Apparently there has been negative information or rumors developed but they have no knowledge of them. However, either participant said they had been assigned tasks that were below their level of competence.

Participant A could not identify any physical problems associated with bullying. But Participant B complained about pain in the shoulders. Both participants said they felt stressed when asked about psychological problems that may result from the bullying; therefore both could develop stress-related illnesses. Participant A attributed cigarette smoking to the bullying which may also lead to greater health problems.

Participant A felt the bullying affected their self-esteem while Participant B Had a totally different response and said the effect would not be allowed. Both participants noted that their supervisors tended to make statements to demean their character performance, which is certainly an indication of bullying. Neither participants has made any career changes. While Participant A has no comments about the role of the organization in creating bullying; Participant B felt bullying is embedded in the organizational culture. Participant B has more direct contact with the management staff and this may have led this participant to have a different view of the organization.

www.ingramcontent.com/pod-product-compliance
Lightning Source LLC
Chambersburg PA
CBHW022052020426
42335CB00012B/657